# THE PHANTOM DEFENSE

# THE PHANTOM DEFENSE

America's Pursuit of
the Star Wars Illusion

Craig Eisendrath, Melvin A. Goodman,
and Gerald E. Marsh,

A Project of the Center for International Policy

Westport, Connecticut
London

**Library of Congress Cataloging-in-Publication Data**

Eisendrath, Craig R.
  The phantom defense : America's pursuit of the Star Wars illusion / Craig Eisendrath,
Melvin A. Goodman, and Gerald E. Marsh
    p. cm.
  Includes index.
  ISBN 0–275–97183–X (alk. paper)
  1. Ballistic missile defenses—United States.  I. Goodman, Melvin A. (Melvin Allan),
1938–  II. Marsh, Gerald E., 1939–  III. Title.
UG743.E36  2001
358.1'74'0973—dc21        2001021159

British Library Cataloguing in Publication Data is available.

Library of Congress Catalog Card Number: 2001021159
ISBN: 0–275–97183–X

First published in 2001

Praeger Publishers, 88 Post Road West, Westport, CT 06881
An imprint of Greenwood Publishing Group, Inc.
www.praeger.com

Printed in the United States of America

The paper used in this book complies with the
Permanent Paper Standard issued by the National
Information Standards Organization (Z39.48–1984).

10 9 8 7 6 5 4 3 2 1

# Contents

# Preface

On May 1, 2001, President George W. Bush made his first presidential address on global issues, announcing that the United States "must move beyond the constraints of the 30-year old Anti-Ballistic Missile Treaty" and must deploy an extensive and expensive shield against nuclear missiles. In the post–Cold War world, the primary enemy against whom a nuclear missile defense would be aimed would not be Russia, but rather "the world's least-responsible states," whom the president did not name. For such states, the president declared, "Cold War deterrence is no longer enough."

While still quite vague on details, President Bush lent his support to a wide variety of missile defense systems, including "technologies that might involve land-based and sea-based capabilities to intercept missiles in mid-course or after they re-enter the atmosphere." He also highlighted the "substantial advantages of intercepting missiles early in their flight, especially in the boost phase," and referred to "promising options for advanced sensors and interceptors that may provide this capability."

It is the thesis of this book that the resurfacing of the "Star Wars" option is not a creative strategy responsive to the threats of what have been called "rogue states" or "states of concern," nor a proper reflection of our status today as the world's only superpower. *The Phantom Defense* takes a hard look at the possible contribution national missile defense might make to U.S. security, by asking the following questions:

Is national missile defense (NMD) technically feasible? The book traces the development of missile defense beginning with the end of World War II, and finds that despite the expenditure of more than $100 billion, making it the most expensive research project in our history, nothing has yet emerged which has even a fraction of the reliability necessary to justify deployment.

The book cites solid reasons why NMD eludes development. Mid-course systems, which hit incoming missiles in outer space, are thwarted by decoys which are indistinguishable from warheads. Boost-phase systems must be too close to launches except in highly selective cases, cannot be carried on U.S. surface ships, and must be fired so quickly that the decision cannot involve deliberation by human beings.

Both systems are decades away from reliable deployment, and the testing of the weapons is highly suspect. The same considerations apply even more strongly with regard to nuclear systems and directed-energy or laser systems. Nor are theater defenses readily convertible to national missile defense.

Is there a credible threat? Here, the Rumsfeld Commission of 1998 fueled the argument for NMD, which is being pressed hard by its author, Donald H. Rumsfeld, now secretary of defense. But the commission's report can be seen as a deliberate attempt to exaggerate a threat with little new evidence; rather it changed the language of earlier studies from statements of remote or tentative probability to sure predictions. When such exaggerations are cleared away, what we find is a very low threat, which could hardly justify launching into a program of such magnitude. Rather, such threats are best handled by a combination of nuclear deterrence and creative diplomacy, not a new arms system.

What will be the geopolitical fallout? Here the evidence is damning. As our friends point out, the system is likely to create a new arms race, increase the missile threat posed by China and Russia, and undo the fabric of arms control agreements which, with deterrence, has radically cut down on nuclear proliferation and prevented a nuclear exchange for over fifty years. It will not provide a reliable deterrent against the so-called "rogue states." Rather than using nuclear missiles, such states are more likely to employ methods of terrorism with other, far less-complicated delivery systems, against which national missile defense is useless. The threat from such states is far more effectively met by creative diplomacy than the deployment of an ineffective missile defense system.

Why does the country continue to pursue national missile defense despite these problems? Since President Reagan beguiled the American public with the illusion of a secure defense against missiles, NMD has appealed to some politicians who see defense as more politically appealing than nuclear deterrence. It also represents a sad truth about the American condition, that once a constituency of defense contractors, laboratories, think tanks, and politicians is created around a particular system, it is difficult to prevent its development or even deployment, no matter how little it may contribute to national security. Such a constituency clearly exists for national missile defense. Others on the right wing of the Republican Party see national missile defense as an opportunity to assert American unilateralism by eliminating treaties that constrain United States freedom of action. Others, romanced by American technology, see NMD as simply the last technical breakthrough.

Finally, the book asks if we will be safer with NMD or without it, and concludes on the basis of overwhelming evidence that far from enhancing U.S. security, NMD will erode it. National security must take precedence over partisan and self-serving politics; national missile defense should be turned down in the national interest.

# Acknowledgments

Although it is impossible to thank the dozens of people who have helped in the preparation of this book, a few have made especially important contributions. We offer our particular thanks to Theodore A. Postol, professor of Science, Technology, and National Security Policy at the Massachusetts Institute of Technology, and perhaps the nation's foremost authority on national missile defense, for making available to us his extensive research on a wide range of technical issues; Joseph Cirincione, a senior associate at the Carnegie Endowment for International Peace, who has generously allowed us to use his material on questions of threat assessment and testing; Professor Richard A. Stubbing, of the Terry Sanford Institute of Public Policy of Duke University, who has advised us closely on the ins and outs of government procurement; and William D. Hartung and Michelle Ciarrocca of the World Policy Institute, who have been particularly valuable in documenting the connections between the arms industry, the political system, and missile defense policy. We also wish to thank Heather Ruland Staines, senior editor of History and Military Studies at Praeger Publishers; Robert E. White, president of the Center for International Policy, and the center's staff, for their constant encouragement and support; and Roberta Spivek for her superb editing.

The views contained in this book are those of the authors and do not necessarily represent the views of the above individuals.

# Introduction

In February 2001, less than three weeks after the inauguration of George W. Bush, his new secretary of defense, Donald H. Rumsfeld, traveled to NATO headquarters in Brussels, Belgium. Rumsfeld told the European members of NATO that the Bush administration was determined to deploy a national missile defense, and the European representatives replied without exception that the United States was moving too fast and that these moves would touch off a new and dangerous arms race (*Washington Post*, February 4, 2001, p. 22). German Chancellor Gerhard Schroeder set the tone of the conference in a keynote speech that warned the United States against "overly hasty and early determinations" in deploying missile defenses. And Karl Lamers, the foreign policy spokesman for Germany's conservative opposition party, the Christian Democratic Union, charged that an anti-missile system was the sort of project dreamed up by people who want to be "invulnerable" so they can be "masters of the world."

The Bush administration appears prepared to ignore the international consensus that a national missile defense would spur a new international arms race, both in Asia and in space, which would create less, rather than more, security. Key European allies initially expressed no interest in Rumsfeld's willingness to "assist friends and allies threatened by missile attack to deploy such defenses." In fact,

U.S.–European cooperation would have negative consequences in Russia, where the Kremlin would presumably decide to retain the multiple-warhead ICBMs that it has agreed to eliminate. Again, the major victim would be strategic stability.

The Europeans clearly believe that a missile defense would come only at the expense of arms control, including the abrogation of the Anti-Ballistic Missile Treaty of 1972. They are particularly concerned with ambitious American plans that look forward to placing weapons in space, which would provoke an arms race that would leave everyone worse off.

One of the most worrisome aspects of the haste of the Bush administration is that none of the technologies needed to produce a national missile defense is currently feasible. Recent tests of land-based defenses have failed, which led to former president William Clinton's decision to defer a decision on deployment of a national missile defense. Sea-based versions being talked of are even further off. No technology can ever be certain of working perfectly, and there is no system the Bush administration could sponsor, including space lasers and enhanced theater defenses, that can be effectively deployed before the administration leaves Washington.

Thus the Bush administration has not only ignored the international opposition to national missile defense but also the arguments that former president Clinton presented on September 1, 2000, when he deferred the decision to deploy such a defense. These arguments emphasized the system's unproven technology, dramatically brought home by a series of failed tests; the unresolved possibility that countermeasures, such as decoys, could foil it; and the objections of Russia, China, and the North Atlantic Treaty Organization (NATO) allies that deployment would jeopardize the 1972 Anti-Ballistic Missile Treaty and the texture of current arms control agreements.

Clinton's proposed system had been advanced to meet pressure brought to bear on his administration by the Republican opposition. When, following its 1994 "Contract with America," the Republican Congress attempted to mandate a national missile defense by 2003, President Clinton vetoed the bill. Clinton then sought to co-opt the issue by devising a "Three-Plus-Three" program, which supported development of a National Missile Defense (NMD) system over three years, and which designated 2000 as the year in which a decision would be made whether to deploy the system over the *following* three years.

The option proposed by Clinton was a system that was designed to counter a limited ballistic missile strike by a country like North Korea or Iran, and which could not conceivably protect the United States from a major ballistic missile strike by Russia or even from a significantly smaller strike by China. For their part, conservatives claimed that their larger system could protect the country against any contingency, although they were notably unclear what their system would entail.

Still virtually untested, President Clinton's proposed hit-to-kill system was even more vulnerable to countermeasures than had been the earlier nuclear-based systems or the Reagan-era space-based technologies. It was also inappropriately designed for use against the stated enemies. As we will see, the proposed system would be inappropriate to deter a terrorist attack; the threat from so-called "rogue states" had been exaggerated; and the system would not be able to protect the country from chemical or biological weapons (see Chapters Four and Five).

Once it became clear that the president's "Three-Plus-Three" system would not work, the Republican opposition began proposing alternatives. These other systems, principally boost-phase and sea-based, contain serious flaws, and, if deployed, would have an equally deleterious effect on our national security (see Chapter Six). National missile defense is simply not an option that is either workable or likely to create its intended effect—the enhancement of U.S. national security.

Originally, as Chapter One details, national missile defense was proposed as a way of countering a possible massive nuclear strike by the Soviet Union. A nuclear exchange with this Cold War rival, with its prospect of one hundred million deaths, was the nightmare scenario that haunted the first planners of an anti-ballistic missile defense system as they began their work in the early 1960s. Their idea was to destroy Soviet nuclear-armed missiles before they could reach the United States. Such a system would provide the United States with a shield, protecting it not only from the missiles themselves, but from the anxieties of the Cold War.

The more scientists and technicians worked on such a system, however, the less feasible it seemed. Every advantage turned out to be on the side of the aggressors. Prototype systems flunked test after test, or passed tests that so greatly simplified their task that success meant little or nothing. No matter how sophisticated the system became, it could not work. It would always be possible for the Soviets in a *real* situation to overwhelm the system by launching too many incoming missiles, and it would always be possible for the incoming missiles to avoid being hit by confusing the defending missiles with chaff and decoys. Finally, the cost of meeting an offensive challenge would always be many times higher than the cost of the offensive challenge itself.

After over a decade of research in the United States and the Soviet Union, both sides recognized the futility of going on with a missile defense system neither side could successfully develop. Pentagon planners also realized that the massive amount of dollars spent on a missile defense system that wouldn't work would drain money away from other systems that the military needed to guarantee U.S. security and protect U.S. armed forces in the field.

Finally, the truth became inescapable. In 1972, President Richard Nixon and Soviet leader Leonid Brezhnev agreed to limit both offensive and defensive missile systems through the ABM (Anti-Ballistic Missile) Treaty. The ABM Treaty forbade both sides from developing a national missile defense system, and did not allow them to do the testing that might make such a system possible. One of the arguments that led to congressional approval of the ABM Treaty, in addition to the fact that anti-missile defense didn't work, was the fear that such a system would provoke the Soviet Union to stoke up the arms race, without increasing U.S. security. In other words, the United States would be worse off with the system than without it. A national missile defense system was like carrying a cap pistol; the other side, thinking it was real, might shoot a real gun first.

Despite bipartisan passage of the ABM Treaty, the Reagan administration took up the cause again in the 1980s, driven by the scientist Edward Teller's and the Livermore Laboratory's overly optimistic claims for a new, nuclear bomb–driven X-ray laser. Then as now, the rationale for a national missile defense system was more political than strategic. As President Reagan knew, a generation of Americans had grown up under the shadow of a possible nuclear war. The doctrine of what had become known as Mutual Assured Destruction (MAD) carried a high moral price; if we could rely on defense, however, we could escape catastrophe. Once President Reagan proposed his Strategic Defense Initiative, or "Star Wars," his approval ratings shot up.

Ultimately, the Reagan administration spent tens of billions of dollars on the development of missile defenses that the vast majority of scientists knew couldn't work, and which were banned by treaty. While President Reagan promised a "nuclear shield" that would achieve an "ultimate security" for the American people, such a system was never even conceivable. Nor was a system feasible that would be limited to protecting the ability of U.S. land-based missiles to survive and retaliate against a Soviet first strike. Whatever such a system's political benefits might be, it was useless in protecting American security.

With the demise of the Soviet Union, the strategic picture has radically changed. Today, no nation can challenge the United States in the way the Soviet Union attempted to do. Today, instead, Americans are told that we need a national missile defense system primarily because our nation is vulnerable to missile attacks from terrorists and from so-called "rogue states," more recently termed "states of concern"—countries like Iraq, Iran, and North Korea. Proponents also argue that while Russia still needs to be considered, a more likely threat is posed by China, which has the capacity to launch a limited missile attack on the United States. Not only nuclear weapons could be involved in such attacks, we are told, but so might chemical and biological weapons, deliverable by intercontinental ballistic missiles.

So far, the United States has spent close to $100 billion in current dollars on various versions of national missile defense, excluding short-term and theater ballistic missile defenses, and has never produced an effective system. If proponents have their way, national missile defense will cost perhaps another $100 billion to $150 billion or more. This enormous expenditure would be better used for more pressing military needs, or for badly needed domestic programs such as education, infrastructure, and the environment.

Although an overwhelming majority of scientists and engineers who have considered national missile defense have deemed it a fantasy, the U.S. government is still pursuing it. What is behind an apparently irrational desire to spend tens of billions of dollars on a system that, after forty years of research, still gives no assurance of working and will erode our security arrangements that do work?

The debate over the wisdom of deploying a national missile defense system has been partly determined by the struggle between two main schools of thought (see Chapter Three). One favors maintaining and strengthening the current global arms control regime, which both

Democratic and Republican presidents have helped create over the last four decades. The other relies on American military might to maintain the nation's option to act at its discretion without moral and legal obligations—a policy of unilateralism. This was the mind-set behind the Senate rejection of the Comprehensive Test Ban Treaty, as well as congressional opposition to the International Criminal Court and the International Land Mines Convention in the late 1990s. It is the rationale driving the building of a missile defense shield, a "Fortress America," from which we can emerge only when and where it suits us.

Behind this belief in unilateralism has been a historical conviction that the United States enjoys a special moral place in the world, and that it has been justified in pursuing policies without international constraints. A second motive has been the American romance with technology. Many Americans believe that any problem is technically solvable, given enough money. For virtually a century, American inventions, from the light bulb to the computer chip, and our ability to translate these inventions into mass production and distribution, have transformed the world. Technology has held out the promise of solving all our problems, provided only that we spend enough money.

Proponents and opponents of national missile defense also view the world in different ways. Proponents see treaty obligations, such as the Anti-Ballistic Missile Treaty, as infringements on U.S. sovereignty, viewing the world as a set of sovereign states. It is a mind-set that looks back to the nineteenth century and before, when populations and economies, protected by national armies, were self-contained. Opponents recognize that today we live in a different world, in a global economy in which manufacturing, financing, and marketing spread over the entire planet. For NMD's opponents, the new world is multilateral, with national authority just one among a number of jurisdictions, regulated by international conventions. In such a world, multilateralism, not unilateralism, holds the key to our true security. Diplomacy and reciprocal obligations, arms reductions agreements, the reduction of regional tensions, and the creation of reasons to cooperate, rather than unilateralism supported by missile defense, are the themes of this new period.

The core group of defense industries, weapons labs, and politicians advocating national missile defense have united their ideological beliefs with self-interest (see Chapter Two). The weapons industries and labs seek to maintain or extend lucrative contracts; the politicians have been rewarded with jobs in their states and districts and with political action committee (PAC) money for their campaigns. Here ideology and self-interest have reinforced each other, providing impetus for a program that for over forty years has failed to deliver.

Why have we written this book? Because we believe the United States needs to seek security in the genuine possibilities of the post–Cold War world, not in the vanishing world of the past. In this scenario, national missile defense, proposed against an exaggerated threat, incapable of being effectively deployed, destructive of arms control agreements, and likely to provoke a new arms race, destroys the national security it is designed to enhance (see Chapter Seven). It is irrational as a policy, and inappropriate as a reward for self-interested groups. Rather than relying on national missile defense, the United States needs to forge the basis for genuine security by moving away from self-serving relationships, and by practicing the creative diplomacy that this period makes possible (see Chapter Eight). Rather than retreat to the past, we need to build for the future.

# PART I

# HISTORY AND MYTHOLOGY

## Chapter One

# Déjà Vu All Over Again: A Short History of "Star Wars"

If no lessons are drawn from the costly experience, if fantasy weapons and other would-be wonders continue to distort federal planning, if science increasingly takes a back seat to politics and private agendas, then the dangers for the nation and the world will inexorably multiply, perhaps to the point of the ultimate calamity.

> From *Teller's War*, written in 1992, by Pulitzer
> Prize–winning *New York Times* reporter William J. Broad

Can anyone tell me again why we need this?

> Trudy Rubin, *Philadelphia Inquirer* columnist, June 7, 2000

The history of anti-missile defense, whether called anti-ballistic missiles, "Star Wars," or the National Missile Defense system is, in Yogi Berra's ironic words, a continuing story of "*déjà vu* all over again." Each segment of that history repeats its predecessors with exasperating similarity:

- First, there are alliances of scientists and weapons laboratories, defense contractors, think tanks, and politicians who are committed to one of several anti-missile systems under research. These usually interrelated groups make unrealistic claims for the systems' early deployment and success, and exaggerate the military threats that the systems are supposed to meet. Through intense lobbying, the alliances, sometimes in competition with each other, gain various degrees of support for their systems from the White House and key sections of Congress.

• Appropriations follow, with huge contracts for the labs and defense contractors, as well as continuing support for the politicians, including contributions to their campaigns and the creation of jobs in their states or districts. As intensified research and testing go on, weapons labs and defense contractors distort the results, and negative findings are politically suppressed. As the systems move toward possible deployment, their potential damage to arms control agreements and foreign relations is also dismissed.

• Eventually, it becomes clear that the systems cannot do what their proponents claimed, and appropriations decrease, although they continue for some time at fairly high rates. By this time, however, several new system ideas are advanced that benefit the same or similar groups of scientists, labs, defense industries, and politicians, and a new segment of the history begins.

The purpose of this chapter is to trace this seemingly unending cycle, focusing on the Reagan and Bush administrations, and to point out the similarities between their history and the Clinton administration, and the possibility that this cycle will continue during the administration of George W. Bush. To slightly rephrase the philosopher George Santayana, we need to ask: If we know the history, why do we need to repeat it?

To set the stage, we return to the beginning of the story, when, at the end of World War II, the Germans rained V-2 rockets on England. While these rockets were terror weapons and were, for the most part, militarily ineffective, they were the first weapons in history against which there was no real defense. A country could fight an army; it could attack bombers or V-1 "buzz-bombs" from the air or shoot them down from the ground; but there was literally nothing England could do to knock out a much faster moving V-2 ballistic rocket. A ballistic missile is a missile that is self-propelled in the launching stage, which then falls freely in its descent to its target. As the technology of ballistic missiles advanced, a multistage intercontinental ballistic missile, or ICBM, with a nuclear, biological, or chemical warhead became capable of hitting targets across a continent or an ocean.

By the mid-1950s, the history of warfare had radically changed. The atomic bomb had been followed by the hydrogen bomb, with a destructive power measured in megatons—that is, in millions of tons of explosives, rather than in the kilotons, or thousands of tons of explosives, unleashed by the kind of bomb that had been used at Hiroshima and Nagasaki. Equally distressing, it was clear that a hydrogen bomb could now be delivered by missiles launched from bases thousands of miles away. As in the case of the V-2 rockets, there was no real defense. The launching pads could perhaps be destroyed on the ground, but once the missiles were in the air, there was nothing to do but await death and destruction.

By the mid-1950s, with the Cold War a grim reality, President Eisenhower began the search for a defense against intercontinental ballistic missiles when he authorized the operational development of a nuclear-tipped interceptor missile, Nike-Zeus, and commissioned Project Defender to develop components for a nationwide ballistic missile defense system. Nike-Zeus was replaced by Nike-X, and was, in turn, replaced by Sentinel. In 1969, President Nixon moved from protecting cities to protecting military sites. Eventually, the Senate approved the deployment of the SAFEGUARD Anti-Ballistic Missile (ABM) system to protect Minuteman missiles at Grand Forks, North Dakota.

Starting in the 1960s, groups of scientists, laboratories, think tanks, and strategists, both political and military, as well as defense industries worked together to support the development and eventual deployment of a full anti-missile defense system. Appropriations funded the research, prototypes were developed, tests undertaken, and claims advanced, often overreaching the verified results.

Many systems were explored. Some models proposed using atomic blasts to destroy missiles, and others would use direct impact; some sought to defend the country as a whole, or specific areas, and others merely the specific launching pads or silos of U.S. intercontinental ballistic missiles. Some would engage the incoming missiles at their launching; others in outer space; and others in the atmosphere near their destination. One of the ideas under development, soon after its discovery in 1960 by Charles Townes, was the concept of a destructive laser. Because missiles traveled at great speeds, more than 12,000 miles per hour, a weapon that traveled at the speed of light might prove more effective in knocking them out than one whose speed was limited by rocket propulsion.

None of these systems, however, proved to be sufficiently convincing, and after over a decade of intensive research, an effective ABM system still seemed highly questionable. In addition, the Partial Test Ban Treaty of 1963 had been approved by the U.S. Senate, so that testing of nuclear-armed interceptors was limited to testing warheads in underground explosions. For the first time, proponents of anti-missile defense were running into the impediment of arms control agreements.

According to prevailing standards of military procurement, a system needed to pass a number of tests to warrant its deployment. It needed to be militarily effective, it needed to be able to survive, and it needed to be cost-effective at the margin, that is, that the incremental increase in defense should not exceed the incremental increase in offense—criteria used by armaments expert Paul Nitze in 1985 to assess the Strategic Defense Initiative (see below). The value of the system also needed to exceed any loss to U.S. security should arms agreements be sacrificed or abrogated, or foreign relations eroded because of the system's deployment. The reader can see in this list the same set of criteria that President Clinton established in 1999 for deployment of the National Missile Defense system. In the mid-1960s, as today, the anti-ballistic missile systems under development failed to meet most of these criteria.

The systems were militarily ineffective because the Soviets, with a growing arsenal of thousands of missiles, could overwhelm them with more missiles than they could conceivably shoot down. Bear in mind that these missiles carried hydrogen bombs, which could wipe out cities. As a protection for the population of the United States, a defensive missile system that purported to defend the population could offer little margin for error. But even as a protection for just U.S. missile bases, to retain the possibility of retaliation in case of a Soviet attack, U.S. anti-ballistic missiles would be inadequate. The other side could still overwhelm American defenses, and, in any case, it could confuse them with various kinds of decoys. Discriminating between decoys and the real warheads, and then shooting them down, would always be many times more expensive than the offensive system. If the United States built a defensive anti-missile system, the Soviets simply could add more missiles or countermeasures to their offensive system, at much lower cost. As Jerome Weisner, President Kennedy's science advisor, and Herbert York, the former director of the Pentagon's Defense Advanced Research Projects Agency, wrote in 1962, building a defensive missile system would goad the Soviets to increase their offensive power, which the United States would then have to match, thus spiraling up the arms race. Rather than gaining security, the United States would face the "dilemma of steadily increasing military power and steadily decreasing national security."

Eventually, the Senate saw that U.S. security would be better advanced by an arms control agreement than by any combination of defensive missile systems, and approved the Anti-Ballistic Missile Treaty in 1972, with only two dissenting votes. The treaty stated in article 5, section 1, "Each Party undertakes not to develop, test, or deploy ABM systems or components which are sea-based, air-based, space-based, or mobile land-based."

The ABM Treaty represented a major arms control achievement that effectively limited ballistic missile defense to a strategically insignificant deployment. It contributed to containing one important area of arms competition by heading off a race in ballistic missile defense. It may also have restrained to some extent the continuing race in strategic offensive arms, although less than was hoped and less than it should have.

The treaty allowed two ABM deployment sites, with one site for each nation's capital and the second at an ICBM field. In 1974, this was restricted to one site by mutual agreement. The Soviet side had been prepared in 1972 to agree not to exercise the right to deploy at the allowed second site, but the United States had been unwilling to go along with this proposal. However, after Congress in 1973 turned down the administration's proposal to deploy ABM defenses in the nation's capital, the question of a second site for the United States became moot. Accordingly, in March 1974, after the Soviet side suggested in talks with Nixon's secretary of state, Henry Kissinger, that both sides renounce the second sites, no one in Washington objected.

The United States indeed built its permitted ABM system, called SAFEGUARD, at Grand Forks, North Dakota, but a year later, after an expenditure of $6 billion, it was dismantled as useless. (The Soviet Union continued to maintain its defense system around Moscow.) Although many in Congress were concerned that the system would be ineffective, vulnerable to attack, and easily overwhelmed, it had been approved in order not to undermine America's negotiating position in the Strategic Arms Limitations Talks (SALT). However, its limitations eventually prompted the House of Representatives to vote for the deactivation of the SAFEGUARD system on October 2, 1975, one day after SAFEGUARD became operational.

Research, however, continued on anti-missile systems, although mostly on defenses of missile silos rather than of the country as a whole. This research kept a number of major American corporations in the game, waiting for the possibility of larger contracts, particularly if systems were eventually deployed.

In this period, leading up to President Reagan's victory in 1980, the main thrust of anti-missile defense research had moved from area defense to point defense of missile silos, and finally to providing a bargaining chip in arms reduction negotiations. The prevailing view of the Carter administration was that U.S. security would depend not on defense, but on deterrence, that is, on the nation's capacity to inflict unacceptable damage on the Soviets even after a first strike, should one occur. This was the system that had come to be known as Mutual Assured Destruction, or MAD, as it relied on the threat of the deaths of tens of millions of people to insure that no side would use nuclear arms. However, the idea of being defenseless while maintaining the capacity to inflict millions of deaths was morally uncomfortable to people on both the right and the left. While MAD seemed to work, an alternative based on defense would have enormous appeal.

Despite the Anti-Ballistic Missile Treaty, which prohibited the United States or the Soviet Union from deploying an anti-missile defense system and had clear limitations on testing one, groups of conservative politicians, defense contractors, scientists, and laboratory and industry representatives assembled to push for anti-missile defenses. A political lobbying group formed in 1978, consisting of politicians, retired generals, and industrialists, called the Committee on the Present Danger, and another related group called High Frontier formed in 1981 to push anti-missile defense. Similar groups had existed in the 1960s and 1970s, although with somewhat less access to the White House. A kind of kitchen cabinet of the Reagan administration, High Frontier was particularly influential, and was able to bypass the usual checks and balances of the U.S. government.

High Frontier was set up by Karl R. Bendetsen, the retired CEO of the Champion International Corporation, and retired Lieutenant General Daniel O. Graham, who had headed the Defense Intelligence Agency. It was soon moved under the institutional umbrella of the Heritage Foundation, a conservative think tank with close ties to the

Reagan administration. In addition, various panels, convened under military auspices, for the study of national security contained a high percentage of corporate members whose businesses stood to gain by favorable findings.

In 1980, the Republican plank called for the United States "To achieve overall military and technical superiority over the Soviet Union," including "vigorous research and development of an effective anti-ballistic missile system, such as is already at hand in the Soviet Union, as well as more modern ABM technologies." Here, the threat of an effective Soviet system was an outright deception; the only system the Soviets had was the totally ineffective one around Moscow, disparagingly called "Galosh," which the United States had dismissed, and evidence was otherwise lacking that the Soviets were honing in on an effective system. At the same time, the Pentagon was claiming that, with Soviet advances in missile accuracy, the U.S. land-based system might well not survive a Soviet first strike, and therefore needed to be defended. Such claims frequently failed to mention U.S. submarine-based missiles, which were virtually invulnerable, as well as the country's formidable fleet of bombers.

High Frontier's Daniel Graham promised that, by using "off-the-shelf" technology, the United States could build a network of several hundred satellites carrying rocket interceptors that would defeat any Soviet attack. He claimed that the United States could launch this system for some tens of billions of dollars. This plan met with nearly universal rejection by defense analysts. In November 1982, Secretary of Defense Caspar Weinberger wrote Graham:

> Although we appreciate your optimism that "technicians will find the way and quickly" we are unwilling to commit this nation to a course which calls for growing into a capability that does not currently exist. While there are many instances in history where technology has developed more quickly than the experts predicted, there are equally as many cases where technology developed more slowly.

Weinberger based his view, in part, on an Air Force Space Division analysis that had concluded High Frontier "has no technical merit and should be rejected. . . . No alternate configuration supported a favorable conclusion." Another Defense Department analysis stated, "It is the unanimous opinion of the Air Force technical community that the High Frontier proposals are unrealistic regarding state of technology, cost and schedule."

The Reagan presidency saw the largest build-up of American arms in U.S. history. In addition to its political motivation, Reagan's claim that the United States was woefully unprepared, his armaments build-up, and his administration's push to develop missile defense systems were the result of a serious misreading of Soviet military spending.

In 1975, preparing for the presidential election the following year, President Ford removed the director of central intelligence William Colby and replaced him with a political appointee, George Bush. Ford and his Foreign Intelligence Advisory Board then appointed a team of right-wing academics and former government officials, headed by Harvard Professor Richard Pipes, to draft their own intelligence estimates on Soviet military power. Pipes had consistently labeled the Soviets an aggressive imperialistic power bent on world domination, and his estimates were drafted in order to reify his views. The group was called Team B, and it predictably concluded that the Soviets had rejected nuclear parity, were bent on fighting a nuclear war, and were radically increasing their military spending. (The committee was called Team B to distinguish it from Team A, the analysts of the CIA who normally performed this type of analysis.) Other members of Team B, particularly Paul D. Wolfowitz, nominated to be Secretary of Defense in the George W. Bush administration, believed that Moscow would use its nuclear advantage to wage conventional war in the Third World. Team B also applied worst case reasoning to predict a series of developments that never took place, including Soviet directed-energy weapons, mobile ABM systems, and anti-satellite capabilities. This mistaken interpretation of Soviet capabilities in strategic defense weapons was used by the Reagan administration to help build support for a costly but ultimately unsuccessful attempt by the United States to develop its own arsenal of nuclear directed-energy weapons.

By 1983, the CIA had corrected their exaggerated estimates of Soviet military spending, but dissemination of this new understanding was suppressed by Reagan's CIA director Robert Gates and defense secretary Caspar Weinberger. This act of making intelligence subservient to policy was an all-too-common feature of Cold War intelligence. Gates also failed to see Soviet President Mikhail Gorbachev as any different from Joseph Stalin—he was simply a communist dedicated to taking over the world and uninterested in any honest effort at arms control—despite mounting evidence to the contrary. Again, one must question present assessments of the irrationality of so-called "rogue states" in the light of such past intelligence readings.

The United States paid dearly in the 1980s for the exaggeration of the Soviet threat and the military build-up at home. It spent over a trillion and a half dollars on defense in the 1980s as the Soviet Union was gradually collapsing like a house of cards; it turned itself into a debtor nation in the process and allowed its education system to erode and its health care system to neglect millions of citizens.

By the end of the 1970s, corporations such as TRW, Boeing, Rockwell International, Lockheed, United Technologies, Textron, and Hughes were heavily invested in laser technology. However, in 1981, the Department of Defense's Science Board concluded unanimously: "It is too soon to attempt to accelerate space-based laser development towards integrated space demonstration for any mission, particularly ballistic missile defense."

Laser technology as the basis for anti-missile defense got a strong boost, however, from a new technology, the idea of X-ray lasers. Its exponents claimed that these lasers, energized by a nuclear explosion, could conceivably destroy all of the Soviets' incoming missiles. The system would be space-based because the X-rays could not penetrate far into the earth's atmosphere. This X-ray variant was pushed by Livermore Laboratory's charismatic Edward Teller, the father of the H-bomb, and an implacable foe of communism. According to Teller, this weapon held the promise of totally reversing the United States' supposed worsening strategic position, and enabling the nation not only to protect its missiles, but its population as well. The United States would move from "mutually assured destruction" to "assured survival."

For several years, Teller and his allies on the Committee on the Present Danger and High Frontier peddled the X-ray laser system on Capitol Hill. High Frontier's Karl B. Bendetsen wrote to Reagan's counselor Edwin Meese that Livermore could deliver "a fully weaponized" X-ray laser "for ballistic defense on a five-year time scale." Despite skepticism from officials at his own laboratory, Teller claimed that a single laser module might destroy more than a thousand speeding missiles by generating as many as 100,000 independently aimable beams. White House interest in the system was also spurred by an alleged "beam gap," indicating that the Soviets were making advances in beam weaponry for missile defense. The "beam gap" was still another instance of how the possibility of a Soviet weapon was, in a worst case scenario, elevated to a virtual certainty.

Eventually, the White House bought the system. As the distinguished physicist Herbert York wrote in 1985, the Strategic Defense Initiative was "an instance of exceedingly expensive technical exuberance sold privately to an uninformed leadership by a tiny in-group of especially privileged advisers." York's use of the word "uninformed" is worth considering. As one reads the history of this period, it becomes clear how scientifically uninformed the political leadership, from Reagan on down, really was, and how easily Teller and others achieved acceptance of technical systems without adequate scientific review. The review process was either politically coopted—for example, Teller had been influential in securing a protégé as the president's science advisor—or was ignored for political reasons. Rather than a government with orderly review committees and clear procedures, Reagan had installed what came close to the British eighteenth-century model of a "king's friends" government of scientifically uninformed advisors.

This group was particularly vulnerable to a mythic figure like Edward Teller, the "father of the H-bomb." It is unclear whether Teller himself consciously deceived Reagan and others, or whether, in his exuberance, he deceived himself, but through his long career he often failed to see the relation between the conceivability of scientific ideas and the possibility of their concrete realization as engineering. That an idea was scientifically possible was no guarantee that it could be developed as an operating system. Teller saw himself as a man with a mission to stop the communists before they destroyed us; his enthusiasm clearly outran the practicality of some of his schemes.

Little was done to increase appropriations for anti-missile systems in the first two years of Reagan's presidency, despite persistent lobbying, and most of the anti-missile funding went into older programs designed to defend missile sites. What finally induced the president to back area defense of the United States, particularly by a nuclear-pumped X-ray laser system, was his political situation. In 1980, Reagan had come into office sharply critical of the Democrats for failing to take a tough line with the Soviets. He then launched the biggest military build-up in U.S. history to close the supposed gap in both nuclear and conventional arms. By the end of 1982, however, there was an economic depression, and public anxiety that perhaps Reagan's aggressiveness was pushing the country into nuclear war. Then, too, a powerful nuclear freeze movement had arisen, and Reagan's land-based missile system, the MX, had proven difficult to base, and temporarily had lost its appropriations.

Reagan's answer was the Strategic Defense Initiative (SDI), or "Star Wars," which looked to defense rather than offense, as in the case of the MX missile, and which could be seen as turning the public image of the president from a warmonger to a man of peace. The Democrats, who backed mutual deterrence, could in this calculus be depicted as the military aggressors. Even though they knew better, Reagan and his administration depicted their proposed anti-missile defense as providing full protection for the population; otherwise, it would have had little political appeal. Reagan even talked of sharing SDI technology with the Soviets, although there was virtually no possibility of this happening. Secretary of State George P. Schultz saw such a system as a way of leveraging Soviet arms cuts, although Teller and Reagan never regarded the anti-missile system as a bargaining chip for arms control, as had Kennedy and Nixon.

Rather, Richard Perle, then assistant secretary of defense for international security affairs, and in 2000 a foreign policy advisor of George W. Bush, saw the Strategic Defense Initiative as a means of doing away with arms control altogether. In this he had the approval of the president, who had a long history of opposing arms control, including the 1963 Limited Test Ban Treaty, the 1968 Non-Proliferation Treaty, the 1972 SALT I Agreement, the ABM Treaty, and the SALT II Agreement in 1979. Both Perle and President Reagan saw arms control as playing into the Soviets' hands and weakening the capacity of the United States to defend itself.

On March 23, 1983, Reagan gave his "Star Wars" speech. He began by asking, "What if free people could live secure in the knowledge that their security did not rest upon the threat of instant retaliation to deter a Soviet attack, that we could intercept and destroy strategic ballistic missiles before they reached our own soil or that of our allies?" President Reagan called on the scientific community "to turn their great talents now to the cause of mankind and world peace, to give us the means of rendering nuclear weapons impotent and obsolete." The president said he was directing "a long-term research and development program to begin to achieve our ultimate goal of eliminating the threat posed by strategic nuclear missiles." He said, "It will take years, probably decades, of effort on many fronts."

The program received no immediate endorsement by the Joint Chiefs of Staff. It is interesting to note that at the time Reagan gave his speech, Air Force officials were on Capitol Hill testifying that space-based laser weapons were insufficiently promising to justify additional funding. General Donald L. Lamberson, the director of the Pentagon's directed-energy programs, told the Senate that he could not recommend an acceleration of the space-based laser program on technical grounds "at this point in time." General Bernard Randolph told the House of Representatives that a laser weapon system would require many megawatts of power; would need a precision mirror much larger than any yet manufactured, which would weigh 150,000 pounds; and that the program would cost "many, many billions of dollars." He explained that "to point the system at a target would be like pointing from the Washington Monument to a baseball on the top of the Empire State Building and hold it there while both of you are moving. . . . I view the whole thing with a fair amount of trepidation."

Nevertheless, two days after the president's speech, National Security Decision Directive 85 gave the ultimate goal of the president's program as "eliminating the threat posed by nuclear ballistic missiles," to be achieved by actions "consistent with our obligations under the ABM Treaty and recognizing the need for close consultation with our allies," which was a patent contradiction.

At first Reagan's speech was ridiculed by scientists and defense experts, and the idea was almost dropped. Two years later, the Strategic Defense Initiative was fully launched and would eventually cost $60 billion. Even before Reagan's "Star Wars" speech, Theodore Postol, then an advisor to the chief of naval operations, pointed out that the technology of a nuclear-powered X-ray laser system was not likely to have any military use for decades. His concerns were dismissed by the administration. Contrary to Postol's sober assessment, numerous defense specialists, policy analysts, and scientists not only eventually fell in line to tell Congress it would work, but predicted deployment within a few years. These assessments contradicted a report to Congress, prepared under the auspices of its Office of Technology Assessment, under the direction of Harvard's Dr. Ashton Carter, which saw the Strategic Defense Initiative as "so remote that it would not serve as the basis of public expectations of national policy on ballistic missile defense," a warning seconded by the Union of Concerned Scientists and other independent experts. A huge 1983 Pentagon report, prepared by Dr. James C. Fletcher, a former NASA director, echoed the president in its summary, but was decidedly less positive in its remaining volumes. Years later, when Fletcher was asked about the inconsistency of the executive summary, he said it was not written by anyone on the committee, but rather by someone in the White House. Fletcher's committee found the X-ray laser futile for defense, as X-rays could not penetrate the atmosphere where fast-burn boosters could be made to operate. The X-ray laser could also be used, if developed by the other side, to destroy all U.S. outer space satellite systems.

Despite these findings, the X-ray laser and several other programs went forward as a massive federal undertaking. The annual budget for ballistic missile defense research quadrupled, from $991 million in 1983 to a peak of $4 billion in FY1988, although the program quickly lost any clear focus. As William J. Broad writes in *Teller's War*, "The federal program of anti-missile research that grew out of President Reagan's initiative had no real focus. It was basically a scientific free-for-all, a license to spend tens of billions of dollars as creatively as possible. Nearly any idea that seemed to show a hint of anti-missile promise was appraised by Pentagon planners and often lavishly funded. No concept seemed too wild." Scores of companies won big contracts, including Boeing, Hughes Aircraft, Lockheed, Rockwell International, and TRW, Inc., many of whom, in the year 2001, are still involved in the development of national missile defense systems.

By early 1984, the Pentagon had created the Strategic Defense Initiative Organization (SDIO), which backed the program, despite initial skepticism. The head of SDIO, Lieutenant General James A. Abrahamson, Jr., responded to criticisms of SDI by saying, "I don't think anything in this country is technically impossible." Caspar Weinberger, the secretary of defense, suggested that it was unpatriotic to doubt that SDI could render ballistic missiles obsolete. (For a discussion of American faith in technology, see Chapter Three.) Despite expert opinion to the contrary, a majority of the public, eager to embrace an alternative to mutually assured destruction, and confident of American technology, bought the SDI program, as Ronald Reagan, "the great communicator," thought they would.

In February of 1985, Paul Nitze, who, in his many years of government service, had served as director of the State Department policy planning staff, secretary of the navy, and deputy secretary of defense, gave a talk in Philadelphia where he enunciated criteria that any anti-ballistic missile system should satisfy. He proposed that SDI should be guided by accepted military standards; and that it should demonstrate military effectiveness, survivability, and cost effectiveness at the margin—that is, that it should be cheaper to add to the defense system than it is for an adversary to add to its offensive weapons. Even SDI proponents conceded, however, that the SDI systems under development could not pass these tests, but pushed for development and eventual deployment anyway.

In the summer of 1987, the SDIO presented to the Department of Defense's Acquisition Board a plan to move from research to the "phased" deployment of strategic defenses. SDI officials advocated the development of a "Strategic Defense System." The Department of Defense approved the new plan, despite the sharp warnings of its own Defense Science Board, which said "there is presently no way of confidently assessing" the system's price or its effectiveness. Thus, SDI proceeded without the usual constraints imposed on any military program, a precedent that has not been lost on those pushing a national missile defense system today.

As for the standard that the system should not make the United States less secure by its effect on arms control agreements, Reagan made clear to Mikhail Gorbachev that he would not accept limits on SDI research in exchange for offensive reductions of weapons. William Broad writes:

> The Reykjavik meeting, which began on October 11, 1986, turned into an extraordinary spectacle of dashed hopes. At the summit, the Soviets, after intense negotiations, offered a grand compromise—the elimination within ten years of all offensive strategic arms, including ballistic missiles, bombers and cruise missiles. In exchange, they wanted SDI limited to the laboratory. But Reagan refused, eager to deploy the system in space. It was one of the most dramatic moments in the history of East-West arms control, holding out the hope of dismantling the weapons that for so long had kept the world poised on the brink of nuclear annihilation. But it passed, unfulfilled, because of Reagan's tenacious grip on his vision.

The United States had already begun to reinterpret the ABM Treaty to permit development and testing of the exotic weapons that it had on the drawing board, including the nuclear-powered X-ray laser. Members of Congress pointed out that the option to reinterpret the treaty rather than an agreement among the signatories to revise or withdraw within the terms of the agreement meant that the United States had unilaterally arrogated to itself the right to rewrite treaties, which would cast doubts on its treaty commitments across the board. Nor, they pointed out, could the executive branch do this without consent of the Senate, which shared responsibility under the Constitution for U.S. treaties. Senator Jesse Helms (R-NC) made the views of the Republican conservatives clear, however, when he called for the deployment of the anti-missile system and for abrogation of the ABM Treaty.

At Livermore and elsewhere, however, development of anti-missile systems was not going well. As early as 1984, it was clear that the X-ray laser was not a viable concept, and the emphasis of the "Star Wars" program was shifted by a presidential directive to "non-nuclear kill" with a "nuclear hedge," although the public did not find out until years later. Despite lack of real progress, and evidence of fraudulent or distorted test results, however, Congress continued to appropriate the money for a variety of approaches. In 1986, 1,600 scientists, many of whom were themselves actually involved in anti-missile research, wrote an open letter to Congress calling SDI a waste of money and a spur to the arms race. Yet administration spokesmen continued to hype the program and, most seriously, delude the president about the results. The appropriations continued. One reason they continued, in addition to the misinformation, may have been political loyalty to Reagan and his "dream"; another may have been the sheer momentum of the effort. As Frances Fitzgerald, the preeminent historian of this period of SDI, writes in her *Way Out There in the Blue*, "Yet, as history has shown, big military programs are rarely canceled once Congress and the contractors are on board."

By the end of 1987, it was clear that the SDI systems under intense development would not even be able to knock out 30 percent of a Soviet first strike. While the Soviets continued to oppose SDI, they were convinced by their advisors, such as the totally credible nuclear physicist Andrei Sakharov, that its basic mission to destroy incoming missiles could not be achieved. The denouement occurred at a meeting between Reagan and Gorbachev in December of 1987.

In his *Master of the Game*, Strobe Talbott records the following conversation:

The President said, "We are going forward with the research and development necessary to see if this is a workable concept and if it is, we are going to deploy it."

Gorbachev answered, "Mr. President, you do what you think you have to do. . . . And if in the end you think you have a system you want to deploy, go ahead and deploy it. Who am I to tell you what to do? I think you're wasting money. I don't think it will work. But if that's what you want to do, go ahead."

The Republican justification of SDI, that it forced increased Soviet military expenditures and so hastened its collapse, seems quite weak in view of the clear evidence that the Soviets had long since ceased to believe, if they ever did, that SDI would work. Far from spending vast amounts of money to counter it, they seemed, for the most part, to have ignored it. Besides, even U.S. intelligence estimates show Soviet spending through the period as flat.

By 1987, the lowered goal of the SDI program was to "reduce Soviet confidence in the military utility of its ballistic missile force" and to "complicate Soviet attack plans." But major technical problems remained and eventually forced reconsideration of even these plans. These are the same obstacles that have ruled out an effective ballistic missile defense for forty years:

- The ability of the enemy to overwhelm a system with offensive missiles;
- the questionable survivability of space-based weapons;
- the inability to discriminate among real warheads and hundreds or thousands of decoys;
- the problem of designing battle management, command, control, and communications system that could function in a nuclear war; and
- low confidence in the ability of the system to work perfectly the first and, perhaps, only time it is ever used or tested under real conditions.

Although George Bush had disapproved of SDI as vice president, in his 1988 presidential campaign he came out for full deployment and reinterpreting the ABM Treaty. However, the technological problems and the exorbitant cost estimates for deploying a full system, reaching over $250 billion, led Bush to reconsider. In January 1991, he abandoned any such plans to protect the nation against a massive Soviet first strike and restructured the SDI system.

Renamed Global Protection Against Accidental Launch System (GPALS), the system was now designed to protect the United States, its forward deployed forces, and its allies and friends from limited ballistic-missile attacks. It would also be compliant with the Anti-Ballistic Missile Treaty. The new system would increase the priority of theater missile defense programs against limited range missiles, and incorporate them into a global system with both ground-based and space-based weapons.

From a peak of $4 billion in 1988, funding of anti-missile research had dropped to an average of $3 billion per year as technology and interest had waned. President Bush's downsizing of the program's mission did not convince Congress to provide funding above that level until the Patriot missile enjoyed its perceived success in the Gulf War in shooting down Iraqi Scuds. (A Scud is a liquid-fueled rocket based on the technology of the World War II V-2 rocket, and is made all over the world.) The Patriot was used to boost funding back up to $4 billion.

Secretary of Defense Dick Cheney told the Senate Armed Services Committee on February 21, 1991:

> Patriot missiles have demonstrated the technical efficacy and strategic importance of missile defenses. This underscores the future importance of developing and deploying a system for GPALS, to defend against limited missile attacks, whatever their source. . . . Defenses against tactical ballistic missiles work and save lives. The effectiveness of the Patriot system was proved under combat conditions.

The SDI director, Henry Cooper, told the Government Operation Committee that year:

> Another observation of the Gulf War is that missile defense can "work" well enough to be extraordinarily useful. . . . In the Gulf War, the Patriot intercepted 51 to 52 Scuds engaged. This level of effectiveness against a very limited threat would be extremely useful whether the offensive missiles were armed with conventional warheads or weapons of mass destruction.

However, Israeli officials and experts disagreed with the army's assessment that the Patriot had succeeded in its military mission. The only debate in Israel was whether the Patriot hit one, or none, of the Scud warheads it attempted to intercept. Israeli officials tracked each

Scud warhead, as well as the debris from the breakup of the missile, upon re-entry into the atmosphere, and thus had the craters to prove that the initial claims of intercept success were false. In the United States, arms expert Theodore Postol wrote in the winter 1991–1992 issue of *International Security*:

> Patriot was misperceived as an "unqualified success." There is no clear evidence that it reduced ground damage in Israel; there is strong evidence that its interceptors failed to destroy a significant number of attacking Scuds; there was a computer failure that caused it not to fire on a Scud that killed more Americans than any other incident in the war; and dramatic video-evidence of Patriot interceptors diving into Israel city streets suggest yet other system failures.

Postol summed it up for the newspapers: the Patriot had experienced "an almost total failure to intercept quite primitive attacking missiles."

In the United States, confusion over the Patriot's performance still fuels overly optimistic estimates of the effectiveness of new, proposed systems. Many officials, journalists, and experts rely on the army report on the Patriot. Yet the army evaluation was performed by a small team of nine officials from the Patriot Program Office and related army offices and others from the prime contractor of the Patriot program, the Raytheon Company. The army, in fact, paid Raytheon $520,000 to provide analysis of Patriot performance in the war.

As a result of congressional investigations into the performance of the Patriot, following Postol's charges, the army revised its claims in 1992 to indicate that the Patriot Missile system had destroyed 52 percent of the Scuds. The General Accounting Office, using the army's own methodology and evidence, suggests that Patriots hit only 9 percent of the Scud warheads engaged, and there are serious questions about even these few hits. The limitations of the Patriot missile system, and the confusion and targeting difficulties caused by the breakup of the Scud-based Iraqi Al-Husayn missile as it reentered the atmosphere, contributed to the high failure rate.

Spending on SDI research continued for the next decade at $3 billion to $4 billion a year. Again, SDI proceeded in defiance of any signal that it was producing deployable weapons, and with clear evidence that it might well tear up the fabric of arms control. In 1991, the very day that Gorbachev and Bush agreed on the Strategic Arms Reduction Treaty (START), Gorbachev attached a statement to the agreement, warning that the Soviet Union might withdraw from START if the United States canceled or violated the ABM Treaty—a position later reiterated by Russian leaders Yeltsin and Putin. The Senate went right ahead and passed the Missile Defense Act, which was signed by President Bush into law. Also, with the Soviet Union breaking up, Bush announced his new set of enemies that SDI would protect us against—rogue states, terrorists, and "narcogangsters," a list which, as we have seen, continues to be cited today.

In addition to the false hype surrounding the Patriot missile, there was a new kid on the block. Its name was "Brilliant Pebbles." This was still another bright idea of the Livermore Laboratory and Edward Teller protégé Lowell Wood, pushed with the same hype. This system envisaged up to one hundred thousand tiny interceptors that could be lifted into space, ready to hit and destroy enemy missiles. Each "pebble" would be an autonomous, child-sized interceptor that would see a ballistic missile as it rose from its launcher, decide whether to engage it, and maneuver into the oncoming path of the missile.

Like its predecessors, "Brilliant Pebbles" failed to live up to its promises. The pebbles became boulders, the cost skyrocketed from $10 billion to $55 billion, just for a first stage, and major problems began to emerge with its performance. Again, the Union of Concerned Scientists critiqued the program, pointing out that offensive forces could easily outwit the system. A General Accounting Office report states that the program research was "mired in software and equipment problems," and that none of the program's technologies were mature enough to support the program. To the objective analyst, none of the SDI concepts—from the X-ray laser to the space-based neutral particle beams to "Brilliant Pebbles"—ever had a prayer of success.

Finally, analysts concluded that with interceptors on each coast, these programs would clearly require abrogation or amendment of the ABM Treaty. While Yeltsin had indicated interest in cooperating with the United States in joint missile defense, he made it completely clear that he would oppose any major revision of the ABM Treaty, and that should the United States unilaterally violate the treaty or attempt to amend it, Russia would take appropriate countermeasures.

Eventually, Bush's program, with official cost estimates running to $85 billion, not including cost overruns, was shelved as being impossible, but again, only after billions of dollars had been spent.

When President Clinton took office in 1993, he quickly broke off ABM Treaty renegotiations with Moscow, reduced the missile defense budget to under $3 billion, and renamed the Strategic Defense Initiative Organization the Ballistic Missile Defense Organization, while leaving program personnel largely unchanged. President Clinton also reversed the program's funding priorities to favor spending on shorter range and forward deployed theater missile defenses over a National Missile Defense system. In so doing, he followed Congress, which had first voiced its preference for theater missile defenses by enacting the Missile Defense Act of 1991. This states that it is "a goal of the United States to provide highly effective theater missile defenses to forward deployed and expeditionary elements of the armed forces of the United States and to friends and allies of the United States."

By 1994, funding for National Missile Defense was relegated to only research programs, with total funding in the low hundreds of millions of dollars. After the Republican party assumed control of Congress in 1995, however, the Congress consistently added funds to the administration's request. In 1996, congressional Republicans proposed the Defend America Act, which would have imposed a National Missile Defense deployment date of 2003. However, the Congressional Budget Office estimated that the proposed system would cost $60 billion, which was too much for a majority in both parties.

Clinton responded with his "Three-Plus-Three" plan, which would demonstrate to Americans that he supported national missile defenses, but disagreed on the timetable for deployment. He also continued research and development of theater missile defenses. As we have seen, the "Three-Plus-Three" plan involved the development of the technology for an anti-missile system within three years, and deployment of a system over the following three years if new missile threats and technology had matured enough to justify this second phase. The plan was to build a missile defense shield over the United States without dragging the United States into serious conflict with the Russians.

The system was to be built in Grand Forks, North Dakota, site of the earlier SAFEGUARD deployment and the only place where a limited national missile defense could be deployed under an exception carved out in the ABM Treaty in 1972. However, these plans were dashed when computer simulations revealed that the proposed single-site system would not protect the westernmost islands in the Aleutians, which were part of Alaska, and some uninhabited islands in Hawaii. Plans were laid for an expanded system, despite the fact that State Department lawyers pointed out that Clinton's proposed National Missile Defense system ran afoul of the ABM Treaty. The political drive to deploy national missile defenses gained momentum with the issuing of official reports, particularly the report of the Rumsfield Commission, which interpreted events in 1998 as indicating a heightened threat to the United States from "rogue states," in addition to China and Russia (see Chapter Four).

As in the Reagan period, tests were rigged or exaggerated, favoring a decision for deployment. In April 1996, however, Nira Schwartz, a computer software expert at TRW, filed a civil suit charging that the company had forced her to misreport her findings about the defensive missile's capacity to discriminate a warhead from a decoy. In using computer programs to certify to the government that TRW's interceptors could pick out enemy missile warheads rather than decoys 95 percent of the time, Schwartz had found that the interceptors could do so only 5 to 15 percent of the time. Such a finding would indicate that the program being developed was virtually useless (for more details, see Chapter Five and Appendix Two).

The companies that were conducting the tests, such as Boeing, Lockheed Martin, and Raytheon, all had a direct interest in their outcome. As *The Nation* correspondents William D. Hartung and Michelle Ciarrocca observed, "The fox is guarding the chicken coop: If Boeing is able to orchestrate a series of seemingly credible tests, it stands to make billions of dollars in production contracts for decades to come. This inherent conflict of interest at the heart of the NMD testing program was one of the factors that have led missile defense experts at MIT and the Union of Concerned Scientists to call for the appointment of an independent panel to assess the feasibility of missile defense before the President makes a deployment decision."

The schedule of tests was also inadequate in comparison with other weapons development programs. The Union of Concerned Scientists pointed out that "the Pentagon expects to test the NMD system less than a typical military system." As in the Reagan and Bush era, corporate control of the testing militated strongly against objective and nonpartisan analysis. Checks and balances involving expert opinion were circumvented, and Congress itself, lacking expertise or the desire to avail itself of it, was presented with findings that flew in the face of scientific facts.

In early 1999, the Clinton administration began pushing to amend the ABM Treaty to allow for a missile defense system that would protect the entire country. In July, the president signed the Missile Defense Act of 1999, which made it U.S. policy to deploy NMD "as soon as it is technologically plausible." The bill included two compromise amendments. One amendment assured that Congress would play a part in determining the system's costs. The other stated that the system must be consistent with policies to reduce Russia's nuclear stockpiles. As he signed the legislation, President Clinton stated that the final decision would be made only after careful consideration as to how the system "would affect our objectives with regard to achieving further reductions in strategic and nuclear arms under START II and START III." The initial deployment, in 2005, would comprise twenty interceptors in Alaska, capable of defending against a limited number of threats from rogue nations. Resources would also be programmed to expand capabilities beyond this, including funding for an additional eighty interceptors by the end of FY2007; an upgraded X-band radar; five upgraded early warning radar facilities; and a larger weapons system complex.

According to an estimate by the Congressional Budget Office (CBO), the first phase of this system would cost nearly $30 billion. The costs for the entire system would total nearly $49 billion through 2015. However, those CBO estimates do not include the costs of space-based sensors for NMD (which would bring the total cost to about $60 billion) because the sensors would be used for other missions as well, and their costs are included in separate Air Force programs. The president's deployment decision was to be based on the maturity of the technology as demonstrated in development and testing, the extent of the threat, likely foreign responses to NMD, and cost. The decision was originally scheduled for June 2000, but then was delayed until September.

On September 1, after two consecutive test failures and widespread opposition to the plan around the world, President Clinton announced, "I simply cannot conclude with the information I have today that we have enough confidence in the technology, and the operational effectiveness of the entire NMD system, to move forward to deployment." The earliest a ground-based national missile defense system could be deployed is now estimated to be 2006 or 2007. Sea-based defenses with at least some capability against long-range missiles could not be fully deployed before 2010 (see Chapter Six).

Department of Defense director of operational test and evaluation Philip E. Coyle III concluded in an August 11, 2000, memorandum that "test results so far do not support a recommendation at this time to deploy in 2005." President Clinton apparently agreed, leading to his deferral, on September 1, 2000, of *any* deployment decision. Director Coyle had also warned, "Deployment means the fielding of an operational system with some military utility which is effective under realistic combat conditions, against realistic threats and countermeasures when operated by military personnel at all times of day or night and in all weather. Such a capability is yet to be shown to be practicable for NMD."

Of the over $310 billion budget for defense programs for Fiscal Year 2001, approximately $4.7 billion was budgeted for missile defense programs managed by the Ballistic Missile Defense Organization. Missile defense remained the single largest weapons program in the defense budget, as it had been for years, accounting for approximately 1.5 percent of the total Department of Defense's budget. With budgets this large, debate over the feasibility and wisdom of deployment is likely to continue for years to come.

Once again, an alliance of scientists and labs, politicians and defense contractors is doing battle for anti-missile systems. Once again, anti-missile defense is being advanced through false claims, ranging from protection of the whole population to a system's ability to protect the country from "rogue states" and terrorists. Once again, anti-missile defense has been made to look more imminently deployable than it is, and claims for its success fly in the face of its clear inability to deal with countermeasures. Once again, potential costs are downplayed, although there is little doubt that if the expanded systems favored by the current Bush administration and by Republican advocates in Congress are put into place, the price tag could be $150 billion or more. Now, as then, the testing has been distorted and sometimes rigged. But the appropriations are still flowing, and will massively increase if a decision is made to deploy. Meanwhile, the entire system of arms control is at risk.

To study the history of "Star Wars" is to go through the same scenario in the past as we see unfolding today. It is unsettling that the United States has spent approximately $85 billion on an unworkable system, and is contemplating spending perhaps $150 billion more, with the risk of irreparable harm to arms control agreements and to the ultimate security of the nation.

## RESOURCES

This short history relies heavily on the exhaustive research displayed in Frances Fitzgerald's superb 592-page study, *Way Out There in the Blue: Reagan, Star Wars and the End of the Cold War* (Simon & Schuster, 2000). Fitzgerald's bibliographic references are also useful. Her focus on the Reagan administration is complemented by William J. Broad's focus on the Livermore Laboratory, one of the primary developers of SDI, and a principal exponent, Edward Teller. See Broad's *Teller's War: The Top-Secret Story Behind the Star Wars Deception* (Simon & Schuster, 1992). See also Janne E. Nolan, *Guardians of the Arsenal: The Politics of Nuclear Strategy* (Basic Books, 1989). Erik K. Pratt's *Selling Strategic Defense: Interests, Ideologies, and the Arms Race* (Lynne Rienner Publishers, 1990) is particularly good on the alignment of forces behind ballistic missile defense. The early history of SDI is told by the Strategic Defense Initiative Organization's official historian, Donald R. Baucom, in his *The Origins of SDI 1944–1983* (University Press of Kansas, 1992). See also "From Nike-Zeus to Safeguard: U.S. Defenses Against ICBMs 1958–1976" by Union of Concerned Scientists (1999) and Stephen Schwartz, ed., *Atomic Audit* (The Brookings Institution, 1999). For the "Star Wars" speech, see President Ronald Reagan, "Peace and Security," March 23, 1983, transcript of television address to the nation, U.S. Department of State, Bureau of Public Affairs, Current Policy Series No. 472.

Raymond Garthoff provides excellent historical material from an insider's point of view in *The Great Transition: American-Soviet Relations and the End of the Cold War* (The Brookings Institution, 1994). For this period, from a Cold War CIA director's angle, see Robert M. Gates, *From the Shadows: The Ultimate Insider's Story of Five Presidents and How They Won the Cold War* (Simon & Schuster, 1996). For an alternative perspective on the role of intelligence, see *National Insecurity: U.S. Intelligence After the Cold War*, edited by Craig Eisendrath (Temple University Press, 2000). See also Strobe Talbott's *Master of the Game: Paul Nitze and the Nuclear Peace* (Knopf, 1988), cited above, and his *Deadly Gambits: The Reagan Administration and the Stalemate in Nuclear Arms Control* (Vintage Books, 1985).

The criteria used by Paul Nitze for the assessment of anti-ballistic missile systems were incorporated into Reagan administration policy as National Security Decision Directive 172, essentially all of which is contained in the unclassified U.S. Department of State Special Report No. 129, dated June 1985. The shift in emphasis of the "Star Wars" program from the X-ray laser to "non-nuclear kill" with a "nuclear hedge" is spelled out in National

Security Decision Directive 119, dated January 6, 1984. The official assessment of the performance of the Patriot is contained in the GAO Report "Operation Desert Storm: Data Does Not Exist to Conclusively Say How Well Patriot Performed," September 1992, NSIAD 920340.

For those interested in the history and details of arms control agreements, see the volumes entitled *Arms Control and Disarmament Agreements: Texts and Histories of the Negotiations*, published by the Arms Control and Disarmament Agency, Washington, DC 20451. For a brief history of national missile defense and a discussion of the complexities involved in reaching a cost figure for national missile defense, see Chapters Two and Five of "National Missile Defense: *What Does It All Mean?* A CDI Issue Brief," September 2000. Copies can be obtained from the Center for Defense Information, 1779 Massachusetts Avenue NW, Washington, DC 20036, *www.cdi.org*. For a discussion of the role of defense contractors in the politics and testing of national missile defense, see William D. Hartung and Michelle Ciarrocca, "Star Wars II: Here We Go Again," *The Nation*, June 19, 2000.

Chapter Two

# Anti-Missile Defense and the Political Maze

At stake in our defense program is not only our national security, but also large opportunities for personal and economic success. ... [The] fundamental reality of the defense game is that each player tends to see his own goals and the national goals as being one and the same, and each plays out the game in accordance with the perceived incentives.

Richard A. Stubbing, *The Defense Game: An Insider Explores the Astonishing Realities of America's Defense Establishment*

The fox is guarding the hen coop.

William D. Hartung and Michelle Ciarrocca, *The Nation*, June 19, 2000

How has it been possible for a military program or set of programs to continue to receive major funding—$85 billion and counting—for more than a forty-year period without the possibility of effective deployment? How has national missile defense continued as a major military program for decades without substantial or enthusiastic support from the military itself? What is it about our governmental system that has lent itself to such a continuing, nonproductive effort?

The answers lie partially in the mechanisms the U.S. political system uses to advance such programs and to fund them. While that system has seen the United States become the dominant military power on the planet, and has produced effective weapons such as the M-1 tank or the F-15 or F-16 fighter bombers, it has also pushed forward programs, such as the B-1 or B-2 bombers and national missile defense, that have had little or no payoff. This chapter attempts to establish that many of the problems encountered in handling national missile defense are endemic to the system of government in the United States, and require long-term generic solutions.

## MILITARIZATION OF INTELLIGENCE AND ITS POLITICAL MANIPULATION

Military intelligence primarily has the mission of assessing the capabilities, both technical and organizational, of potential adversaries. As a result, it tends not to perform the analyses that could minimize or pose alternatives to military force, such as arms control, diplomacy, or foreign economic aid, which it is not set up to analyze. Intelligence in these areas tends to be the responsibility of intelligence agencies not directly under the Department of Defense, such as the Department of State or Central Intelligence Agency. If diplomacy or economic aid might represent a viable policy, as opposed to military force, it is unrealistic to expect those who produce military intelligence to champion it.

Such intelligence, then and now, has had the effect on policy makers of minimizing arms control agreements and diplomacy in favor of military or paramilitary actions. Recent missile programs in Iraq and North Korea, for example, have led to calls for the building of national missile defense. In both cases, however, it was multilateral actions, both military and diplomatic, that proved effective in achieving a suspension of missile tests. In Iraq, the verification regime of the United Nations, before it was compromised by the CIA's penetration of UNSCOM, the UN's inspection team, led to the identification and destruction of more Iraqi strategic weapons than had the military campaigns of Desert Storm. While such lessons should create precedents for greater consideration of nonmilitary options, with the intelligence system currently being dominated by the military, and with the political subversion of intelligence, they may have little effect on subsequent practice. Should the CIA director continue to be politically compliant, the tendency to politicize intelligence is likely to continue.

Today, the nonmilitary components of the U.S. intelligence community are very small, and often overruled. The militarization of intelligence is a far more serious problem today than it was twenty or even ten years ago. Today, almost 90 percent of the entire intelligence apparatus, a figure not including the CIA, is under military auspices, commanding a budget in excess of $27 billion a year. Since the CIA's failure to provide timely and relevant intelligence during the war in the Persian Gulf in 1991, the Pentagon has taken control over most of the intelligence community and weakened the intelligence community's ability to serve as an independent and objective interpreter of foreign affairs, and particularly has weakened the intelligence community's ability to suggest alternatives to military force. A particularly poignant example is the downgrading of intelligence's previously important role of verification and monitoring of arms control and disarmament. For the first time in thirty years, the director of Central Intelligence testified to Congress that the intelligence community could not monitor a strategic arms control agreement— the Comprehensive Test Ban Treaty, which contributed to the Senate's refusal to confirm it. The decision to testify in this manner would seem to be based more on political considerations than on technical ones, as the United States certainly has the ability to monitor all militarily significant tests, that is, those that exceed several hundred tons of yield.

The militarization of intelligence has other serious consequences. A militarized intelligence community, and the services seeking funds, tend to overestimate threats, and then ask for more than is needed to meet them. Such assessments are, to some extent, understandable as it would seem preferable for the Defense Department and the military services to run the risk of having too much or even of acquiring marginally useful defense systems than be outmatched on the battlefield. If there is uncertainty, better to err on the side of excess. Such exaggerations of threats, however, make it easier to convince a generally sympathetic Congress to appropriate funds, and can be used by congressional groups that may have agendas of their own (see below). Faced with a situation in which American troops are depicted as being vulnerable in the field, Congress can generally be counted upon to come up with responsive funding. This is even truer if Americans can be depicted as being vulnerable in their homes—the picture Americans have been given of their situation should "rogue states" or, incredibly, even terrorists acquire long-range missile capability (see Chapter Four).

The political manipulation of intelligence has provided modern history with disturbing gaps such as the "bomber gap" of the 1950s and the "missile gap" of 1958–1961, which depicted the United States as being vulnerable to supposed Soviet military superiority. Here it should not be forgotten that it was the CIA's then independent imagery analysis that determined that there was no "bomber gap" between the Soviet Union and the United States in the 1950s and no "missile gap" from 1958 to 1961. Independent CIA imagery analysts successfully battled the Department of Defense on sensitive military issues in the late 1960s and the early 1970s and, as a result, CIA analysis eventually contributed to the first SALT agreement and the Anti-Ballistic Missile Treaty in 1972. In both cases, the White House had to guarantee to the Senate that the intelligence community could verify and monitor the disarmament agreements.

Once intelligence, however, becomes politicized, we find distortions such as the inaccurate estimate of the Soviet arms build-up in the late 1970s leading to the staggering Reagan military budgets in the early 1980s. As we will see in Chapter Four, such contemporary exaggerations have resulted in the remote possibilities of a North Korea or Iran producing missiles that can reach the United States becoming virtual certainties.

## DEFENSE IN CONGRESS

Compounding the problems created by the militarization of intelligence, and particularly its political manipulation, have been problems stemming from the way defense questions are handled in Congress. The defense budget, for example, is considered with virtually no relation to funds devoted to other areas of national security, such as international security assistance, economic assistance, diplomacy, or even, to some extent, intelligence. Rather than seeing the entire package together, and trading the relative effectiveness of dollars in one area over another, Congress takes up defense as a separate, hermetically sealed item. This problem is compounded by the fact that, within Congress, different committees handle different programs, again making coordination difficult.

Perhaps even more seriously, Congress has opted for a budget in which well over 90 percent of the national security budget is directed to military programs, and if military assistance is included, only about 1 percent of the budget is concerned with other areas. Nevertheless, where Congress has increasingly involved itself in deciding the levels of the nondefense areas of the national security budget—and recently, most often in a negative way—it has generally been unwilling to take a hard look at the overall defense budget levels and the best mix of programs to meet realistic threats.

This system has resulted in a lopsided reliance on military defense as opposed to other means. The United States gives only one-tenth of 1 percent of its Gross National Product in economic aid, and ranks at the bottom of sixteen industrial nations in development assistance as a proportion of its GNP. As countries such as India, China, North Korea, Iran, and Iraq become relatively poorer year by year than the United States, as measured by average income, the unwillingness of the United States to respond to these conditions becomes a liability that inevitably affects its security.

Think what a difference a few billion dollars might make, in comparison with a $310 billion defense budget, in providing economic aid to areas of the world that might pose possible threats now or in the future. Today, for instance, North Korea has a total military budget of $2 billion, and is decidedly in difficult straits economically, and yet a possible North Korean missile attack is given as a major justification for a U.S. missile defense system that might cost us up to $150 billion dollars. It is not difficult to imagine that North Korea's interest in building missiles might well be blunted by an economically advantageous relationship with the United States, one that would not necessarily bolster its dictatorial regime.

To give another example, for the last few years the United Nations was partially crippled by the United States withholding regular and special peacekeeping dues. Full payment, and perhaps the use of additional funds to create the basis of an effective UN rapid deployment force, would have created substantially more benefit for U.S. national security than would the tens of billions of dollars projected for a national missile defense system, or for the continued building of questionable new weapons systems, such as additional nuclear submarines, for which there was no justification in the post–Cold War world. A compartmentalized budget and the preoccupation of Congress with levels of nonmilitary UN security expenditures have prevented such comparisons or tradeoffs.

The preference for military over diplomatic solutions, including agreements to reduce missiles and to prevent the proliferation of nuclear, chemical, and biological weapons, has also been exacerbated in recent years by the eclipse of the State Department as a policy-making agency in favor of the intelligence and military systems. Funding for the operation of the State Department, now at approximately $2.3 billion a year, is less than 1 percent of the Department of Defense budget, and hundreds of millions of dollars lower than that of the Central Intelligence Agency. While intelligence, now funded at over $30 billion a year, and Defense, set at over $310 billion, enjoy high congressional support, the State Department has year by year lost funding. This has meant not only the closing of over thirty embassies and consulates in recent years, but the increasing reliance of the State Department on the use of CIA operatives in diplomatic positions. In its weakened position, the State Department has been unable to advance diplomatic options as opposed to espionage and covert action, often favored by the intelligence system, or reliance on the threat of military force, as posed by the country's overwhelming military superiority.

## POLITICS AND NATIONAL SECURITY

Threat exaggeration and the political manipulation of intelligence can serve not only the party in power, but also the party seeking power, with a politically effective charge that its rival in office is not doing its job. Ronald Reagan, for example, in need of a political issue, created a virtual media blitz to propagate his notion that the United States was in imminent danger because of Soviet military superiority, justifying the greatest increase in U.S. military spending in our history, an increase that eventually included the Strategic Defense Initiative. Inaccurate and politically manipulated statistics became "missile gaps" and "beam gaps." The result was a picture that seemed to give the Soviets a disturbing edge in military strength. Yet, as we now know, increases in Soviet defense spending never presented even remotely the dangers that Reagan administration spokesmen evoked. Yet between 1976 and 1981, a Gallup survey reported that the percentage of Americans who thought that the United States was spending too little on defense went up from 22 percent to 51 percent, thereby creating political pressure on Congress to vote up appropriations and, as part of this picture, to support the Strategic Defense Initiative.

As will be seen, threat exaggeration and the political manipulation of intelligence were again at work as a militant Republican Congress pressured the Clinton administration to deploy an expanded national missile defense. Here, also, politically tendentious commissions and reports played their part. The most prominent was the 1998 Rumsfeld Commission, established by Congress to "assess the nature and magnitude of existing and emerging ballistic missile threats to the United States." Donald Rumsfeld, former Secretary of Defense in the Ford administration, was hardly unbiased, being a contributor to the Center for Security Policy, the most prominent lobbying group pushing for national missile defense today. It was the Rumsfeld Commission that stated in July 1998, for example, that within five years North Korea could develop a missile capable of reaching the United States, an estimate significantly shorter than that of the CIA. According to physicist and commission member Richard Garwin, the final report distorted the findings of the commission concerning North Korea and the threat posed by other countries to fit the Republican political agenda. "I am alarmed that some have interpreted our findings as providing support for a new national defense system," Garwin noted. Partially based on the Rumsfeld report, the Senate and House passed bills in March of 1999 calling for anti-missile deployment "as soon as it is technologically possible."

Again, repeating policies of the Reagan era, the Clinton administration sought a massive increase in military spending, $112 billion over six years, in response to Republican electoral charges rather than the U.S. strategic position. As the *London Financial Times* made clear (July 3, 2000), "As for Mr. Clinton, his paramount desire is not to leave Al Gore, the Democratic banner-carrier, looking softer on defense than George W. Bush, the Republican front-runner and proponent of NMD." With both candidates favoring a military build-up, defense, including an anti-missile system, was not a decisive issue in the November 2000 election.

## ECONOMIC BENEFITS OF NMD

Clearly, one reason members of Congress have not attacked the overall figure for defense, and have advanced particular programs whose contribution to national security may be dubious, is because of economic benefits for their constituents and for themselves. Defense industry spending provides income for over ten million Americans, or approximately one-tenth of the workforce, particularly in the south and west. These, not unexpectedly, are the areas most strongly represented on the appropriate congressional committees, and particularly in their chairmanships. Because members of Congress think it is their duty to "bring home the bacon" to their constituents, defense contractors establish production facilities and let subcontracts in states that provide these contractors the desired allocations.

The history of the B-1 bomber illustrates this tactic, although the B-2 bomber, with no discernible mission, could equally well be cited. In 1977, President Carter opted not to build the B-1 bomber because of its dubious effectiveness and high cost. Nevertheless, individual congressional members and staffers of the defense committees were able to end-run Carter and provide the program sufficient funds to keep it alive until the Reagan presidency. In 1981, despite the fact that Soviet air defenses were expected to threaten the B-1's penetrating capability by 1990, the Reagan administration opted to reinstate it. Nevertheless, its $30 billion price tag made it controversial, as did support for the competing Stealth bomber. The Air Force and Rockwell, which had been awarded the B-1 contract despite little experience in bomber construction, met this challenge by awarding contracts to subcontractors in forty-seven states. With such support, the B-1 sailed through Congress, and became a major weapon system.

Internal politics rather than national security needs often dictate appropriations in another way as well. Each year, billions of dollars of unneeded or "pork" appropriations are added to the defense budget. As Senator Thomas Eagleton, a Democrat from Missouri and former member of the Defense Appropriations subcommittee, explained, "In committee, you sometimes feel: Well, put a few hundred million here and maybe that'll buy us some peace and quiet within this guy, and give a contract out here and that'll satisfy Congressman so-and-so. It's not a superb way to fashion a defense budget."

For their part, large defense contractors maintain substantial offices in Washington. These are often staffed by retired military officers who, after relatively early retirements, go on to careers as congressional staffers and lobbyists for defense industries, while maintaining their contacts with their former employers. Through such revolving-door arrangements, the armed services, Congress, and defense contractors maintain tight relationships based on personal loyalties, which, again, may have little to do with the national interest. Legislation forbidding such relationships has been, for the most part, ineffective.

The indirect benefit of increased employment in congressional districts is supplemented by direct and indirect payments to members of Congress from the defense contractors. The lobbying offices maintained by the Washington offices of aerospace industry contractors are the conduit for these political action committee (PAC) payoffs. These lobbying offices, with dozens of employees, are some of the largest in Washington.

Unfortunately, the U.S. government system cannot run without them. Today, it costs roughly $10 million to run for the U.S. Senate, with the price rising year by year. In the absence of any effective campaign finance reform legislation—the United States is the only major industrial country in the world without it—this money must be raised from outside sources, as a senator's salary is only a small proportion of the total needed. This situation makes American legislators particularly vulnerable to PAC funds. It is no coincidence that the same forces in the Congress, headed in 2000 by Senator Trent Lott, that backed national missile defense opposed campaign finance reform legislation. Given this situation, contracting procedures are, in the words of Richard Stubbing, a professor at Duke and formerly with the Office of Management and Budget, "partisan, politicized, and occasionally corrupt."

Another reason for such favoritism, in addition to PAC payoffs, is that Congress wishes to maintain the health of companies in local districts, and both Congress and the Pentagon wish to maintain an industrial base in case of war. An example is the 1976 intervention of President Ford's Secretary of Defense Donald Rumsfeld on behalf of Chrysler, a Michigan corporation, in its competition with General Motors for the multibillion-dollar contract for the M-1 tank. The contract award, which had every appearance of bias, earned Chrysler $60 million in profits per year at a time when its automobile sales were consistently losing money. Studies, such as those by Richard Stubbing and more recently by William D. Hartung and Michelle Ciarrocca at the World Policy Institute, document the extraordinary coincidence of the location of awarded contracts, PAC donations, and the districts of key legislators.

## QUALITY CONTROL PROBLEMS

National missile defense, as in the case of other dubious military programs, is seen by defense industries as a continuous source of support, in addition to such measures as streamlined export rules, relaxed auditing, and subsidies. While it is not in the nation's interest to have these contractors go out of business, they should be held accountable through good government contract management.

Defense contracting procedures, as in other industries, favor a company that comes in at a low price and promises high performance and early delivery. Once a contract is awarded, however, the company is in a monopoly position. When the price goes up and the delivery date is postponed, penalties are rarely imposed because there is often no other company ready to step in. Here members of Congress generally resist imposing penalties for industries in their states or districts that also provide direct financial contributions and provide their constituents with jobs. Once in production, the company continues to benefit for a period of ten to twenty years by highly profitable sales and service contracts. In addition, the time it takes to move weapon concepts off the drawing board and into production has increased dramatically, although the penalties for such extensions have been mainly nominal. With such procedures, it is difficult to demand quality performance, or to invoke penalties for poor performance or cost overruns.

Finally, there are specific characteristics of military projects that make quality control difficult. Detailed specifications for military weapon systems are often classified and restricted to authorized personnel in U.S. agencies or their contractors. Although there are very good reasons for this practice, it also makes it very difficult to monitor contractor performance. Review panels are a good approach, but their independence is frequently questionable.

Bad management or lack of proper oversight can result in outrageous costs, as more and more money must be spent to bring a system up to specification. It can produce weapons that have no real military purpose, such as the B-2 bomber, originally designed for a nuclear penetration mission into the Soviet Union. This was rendered unnecessary by cruise missiles that could be carried by B-52s without their entering Soviet airspace. Finally, secrecy and closed access facilitate misrepresentation to members of Congress, the executive branch, and the public, who often have no access to outside assessment.

## LOBBYING FOR NMD

The political system, then, seems particularly vulnerable to alliances of politicians, defense contractors, think tanks, and politicized scientists. We have seen how such alliances worked in the Reagan period to push "Star Wars." The alliance group that is presently most prominently pushing national missile defense is the Center for Security Policy, headed by Frank Gaffney, who had been Richard Perle's assistant when Perle was assistant secretary of international security affairs under President Reagan. According to Frances Fitzgerald, Gaffney had become "a one-man SDI lobby." (Perle, a major foreign policy advisor for George W. Bush during the 2000 presidential campaign, has continued actively pushing national missile defense.) It was Gaffney who persuaded Newt Gingrich to include in his 1994 "Contract with America" a provision "requiring the Defense Department to deploy antiballistic missile systems capable of defending the United States against ballistic missile attacks."

In the fall of 2000, Gaffney's Center for Security Policy included on its advisory board Ed Feulner, president of the Heritage Foundation, and Henry Cooper of High Frontier, the "Star Wars" think tank of the Reagan period. Other members included Charles Kupperman and Bruce Jackson of Lockheed Martin; Senator John Kyl (R-AZ) and representatives Curt Weldon (R-PA) and Christopher Cox (R-CA); Edward Teller; and Reagan's former science advisor George Keyworth, a Teller protégé. Boeing, Lockheed Martin, Raytheon, and TRW, which hold over 60 percent of the present National Missile Defense contracts for a total of $2.2 billion in fiscal year 1998 and the first three-quarters of fiscal year 1999, are major contributors to the center. This coalition of politicians, defense contractors, and think tanks exactly replicates such lobbying groups as the Committee on the Present Danger and High Frontier, which sold Congress and the White House on anti-missile defense in the Reagan era.

The influence of lobbying groups on National Missile Defense is well documented by William D. Hartung and Michelle Carrocca in the June 19, 2000, issue of *The Nation*. They report: "World Policy Institute analysis of two recent pro–Star Wars letters to President

Clinton—one from twenty-five senators organized by Jesse Helms stating that they would kill any arms-control deal with the Russians that attempted to put any limits on the scope of future NMD deployments, the other from thirty-one Republican senators pushing the Center for Security Policy's pet project, a sea-based missile defense system—reveals that the signatories of these pro–Star War missives have received a total of nearly $2 million in PAC contributions from missile defense contractors in this election cycle." Hartung and Carrocca report that Lockheed Martin, Raytheon, Boeing, and TRW spent $34 million on lobbying during 1997–1998. They also report that from 1997 to May of 2000, these four corporations "kept up a brisk pace of political giving, doling out more than $3.7 million in PAC contributions to members of Congress. Soft money contributions by the four major missile contractors, which go to the parties, are running at $2.1 million for the same period."

These patterns, which are decades old, have provided the template for National Missile Defense. If we compare how this system is currently working, we will see the same patterns unfolding as noted in the previous chapter.

- As in the history of SDI and the Reagan era, intelligence is manipulated for political ends, and "worst case" threats are being presented. This creates a favorable political climate for a system like National Missile Defense, which sober analysis reveals to be both unnecessary and unworkable (see Chapter Five).

- Nonmilitary approaches to international tensions, such as economic aid, arms control arrangements, and diplomacy, are minimized, and resources denied.

- The push for the weapons system comes more from the political sector than the military. As in the past, tendentious commission findings play a prominent role.

- The defense budget dwarfs all other approaches to foreign affairs, and is pushed not only for its contribution to national security, but for its economic effects on political constituencies, and because of defense industries' political contributions.

- Members of Congress concern themselves with maintaining the viability of defense industry corporations to the detriment of the sound management of defense contracting. Management and supervision procedures are often lax, allowing delays and cost overruns.

- National Missile Defense, as in the case of other dubious programs, is being pushed by a lobby group that represents an alliance of politicians, defense contractors, think tanks, and politicized scientists that the system allows to have virtually unregulated power.

What we see in this recital is not only a repeat of the events of the Reagan and Bush periods, but also illustrations of endemic problems in the American political system that cry for correction. These problems strongly militate against objective, well-informed assessment of U.S. strategic needs, and help make possible the continuing saga of support for a defensive system that does not work, wastes valuable resources, and actually erodes national security.

## RESOURCES

This chapter draws heavily on a seminal work by Richard A. Stubbing, with Richard A. Mendel, *The Defense Game: An Insider Explores the Astonishing Realities of America's Defense Establishment* (Harper & Row, 1986). Reporting by William D. Hartung and Michelle Ciarrocca, some of which appears in their article in *The Nation* on June 19, 2000, "Star Wars II: Here We Go Again," provides a contemporary confirmation of Stubbing's findings. Other useful data are reported by Hartung and Ciarrocca in Internet publications of the World Policy Institute.

Analysis of the U.S. intelligence system is provided in Melvin A. Goodman's "In from the Cold: The Need for Reform of the CIA," in *International Policy Report*, June 2000, published by the Center for International Policy; and in his chapter, and those by Robert E. White and Richard A. Stubbing, in *National Insecurity: U.S. Intelligence After the Cold War*, edited by Craig Eisendrath (Temple University Press, 2000). For an analysis of the federal budget and the funding of nonmilitary programs, see Richard N. Gardner, "The One Percent Solution," in *Foreign Affairs*, July/August 2000.

For a detailed, expert analysis of how arms control policy is what Strobe Talbott calls "policy made and remade in response to politics," see his *Deadly Gambits: The Reagan Administration and the Stalemate in Nuclear Arms Control* (Vintage Books, 1985). The book is also instructive in depicting the intense competition in arms control policy-making between the State Department and the Department of Defense. For a set of important essays on the arms control process, see *World Security: Trends & Challenges at Century's End*, edited by Michael T. Klare and Daniel C. Thomas (St. Martin's Press, 1991).

For an English account of national missile defense, see the *London Financial Times*, July 3, 2000.

## Chapter Three

# Two Views of the World

Wee shall be as a Citty upon a Hill, the eies of all people are uppon us; soe that if wee shall deale falsely with our god in this worke wee have undertaken and soe cause him to withdrawe his present help from us, wee shall be made a story and a by-word through the world.

John Winthrop, 1630, as quoted in Daniel J. Boorstin, *The Americans: The Colonial Experience* (Random House, 1958)

To study this period is to reflect upon the extent to which our national discourse about foreign and domestic policy is not about reality—or the best intelligence estimates of it—but instead a matter of domestic politics, history and mythology.

Frances Fitzgerald, *Way Out There in the Blue: Reagan, Star Wars and the End of the Cold War*

To be sure, there is nothing wrong with doing something that benefits all humanity, but that is, in a sense, a second-order effect. America's pursuit of the national interest will create conditions that promote freedom, markets, and peace.

Condoleezza Rice, in *Foreign Affairs*, January/February 2000

With the end of the Cold War, the United States emerged as the world's only superpower, a position it may well hold for some decades. What the nation chooses to do with this power is up for question. Some, like former president George Bush or George W. Bush's national security advisor, Condoleezza Rice, believe it is the role of the United States to attempt to maintain and extend an encompassing world order, a set of laws and arrangements that the United States defines or selectively chooses to adhere to, that serves the U.S. national self-interest, and that, incidentally, may benefit other nations. In this sense, the United States remains the principal guarantor of this post–Cold War order. The uniquely powerful economic and military status of the United States incurs a responsibility to protect this order; no one else can.

According to this view, the base from which the United States creates this unilateral set of options is its territorial borders, which sharply distinguish it from every other nation. National Missile Defense is then seen as a vital means of protecting the national territory from attack by other states—and even, some claim, from terrorists. For some proponents, NMD also means the extension of this protection to the United States' closest allies in the developed world.

In this mode of thought, the United States can do the most for itself and for the rest of the world by not allowing the current arms control regime and other obligations to inhibit its freedom of action. Treaties that impose constraints on U.S. power must then be dismantled. It is therefore no accident that those who support a national missile defense also oppose the Anti-Ballistic Missile Treaty, the Strategic Arms Reduction Treaties (START), the Non-Proliferation Treaty, the Outer Space Treaty, and other such instruments of arms control. Despite the fact that the arms control regime has helped prevent nuclear conflict throughout the Cold War, it is now time, this group contends, to abandon it. As for initiatives presently on the table, such as the Comprehensive Test Ban, the International Criminal Court, the International Land Mines Convention, or a ready deployment force by the United Nations, the group's answer is the same: the United States should in no way inhibit its unilateral power to act.

This unilateralist position has been stated clearly by William Kristol and Robert Kagan, for instance, who maintain that "the United States can and should lead the world to a better future, one built around American principles of freedom and justice—but only if it has the power and the will to use that power. . . . American dominance can be sustained for many decades to come, not by arms control agreements, but by augmenting America's power and, therefore, its ability to lead." For such men, including their conservative allies in Congress, arms control represents a "Cold War mentality." As reported in the *New York Times* of January 12, 2001, Donald Rumsfeld "derided the Anti-Ballistic Missile Treaty of 1972 . . . as 'ancient history.' " On May 1, President Bush declared, "This treaty does not recognize the present or point us to the future. It enshrines the past."

The cardinal sin of these treaties, for the president and others of his frame of mind, is that they restrict U.S. freedom of action. By the same token, national missile defense manifests our freedom to protect our own citizens from attacks by those who may not appreciate U.S. hegemony and the international order it attempts to maintain. This world view has the power to capture the imagination, as it did in the Reagan period. Who would not want to protect the American people from attack? Who would not want to use America's historic opportunity to peacefully extend its power and influence around the world to advance freedom and justice?

## GLOBALIZATION OR THE NATION STATE?

In considering the exercise of unilateral American power, it is good to think of the words of Edmund Burke, who wrote at the apex of British power at the end of the eighteenth century: "I dread our own power and our own ambition; I dread our being too much dreaded. . . . We may say that we shall not abuse this astonishing and hitherto unheard-of power. But every other nation will think we shall abuse it." The situation against which Burke inveighed was that of England assuming hegemony in a world of sovereign nation states. The sovereign state came fully into its own in the seventeenth century, signaled by the Treaty of Westphalia in 1648, which ended Europe's religious wars and saw the final break-up of a universally Catholic Europe. No longer were territories ruled by multiple jurisdictions of empire, nationality, fiefdom, church, and holy orders, united by a common language and a common religion. Rather, a new system was established of separate and exclusive sovereignties. Each nation had its self-contained economy and society, laws, clear borders, national church, bureaucracy, and armed forces that protected them. From that base, at the end of the eighteenth century, England, whose navy was the terror of the seas, could dream of establishing English hegemony, a Pax Britannica of English law and English economics for Indian, Hottentot, and Irishman alike; it could look to a future of English economics and the English language covering the globe. The vision of American hegemony offered by the pundits of unilateralism looks little different from the dreams of Englishmen over two hundred years ago.

This is hardly a modern or progressive view of the world. An opposite view is implicit in the observation of social planner Felix Rohatyn: "Economic policy and national security policy are related to each other, depend on each other, and must be considered as worldwide in scope." The basis for such a policy is not the nation state, such as England or the United States, but the world community.

For the first time in centuries, the economic unit and the territorial national political unit are no longer identical. Globalization, the phenomenon of the internationalization of production and the unprecedented growth of a worldwide financial market, has subsumed the nation state. U.S. territorial borders may end at Mexico or Canada, but the financing, ownership, production, and sales of transnational corporations are oblivious of national frontiers. Jurisdictions are also becoming transnational, whether for environmental controls, human rights, intellectual property rights, or the maintenance of world peace.

Equally so, notions of national security that look exclusively to the interests of the nation state make progressively less sense as we move into this new era. The argument that the United States must alone determine everything that affects its citizens, that its sovereignty is absolute, flies in the face of the new realities. The go-it-alone view of those who support national missile defense and the dismantling of arms control agreements and organizations like the United Nations— what they call "utopian internationalism"—looks backward to a world that is rapidly disappearing. Advocates of this view appear to see the modern global economy as an agglomeration of national economies similar to those of the nineteenth century, when mainly British, French, and Dutch business empires had foreign branches that were almost exclusively involved in the distribution and marketing of products made at home. Even if the American people had the stomach for the ruthlessness of nineteenth-century imperialism, such economic conditions no longer exist in today's interdependent global economy.

## MUTUAL DEPENDENCE IN A DANGEROUS WORLD

In such a world, the United States' first option for defense should be the strengthening of relations that facilitate mutual security and that make its extension more advantageous. Attacks against the United States, and particularly the use of weapons of mass destruction, will only be acts of desperation. Because such acts against the world's remaining superpower would be national suicide, they are avoidable through diplomacy and economic initiatives. Attributions of madness or total irrationality to potential enemies is a form of cultural snobbery that a nation can ill afford. Diplomacy and negotiation are ready options. The vast power, both military and economic, that the United States indeed possesses can here be used to facilitate the move to diplomacy and to further conditions of mutuality that make such attacks unthinkable.

This is the world toward which we should be heading. The aim of the United States should be to extend those instruments of international policy embodied in the arms control regime that make such a world a safer place. This is the regime that has kept the number of nuclear states to a manageable figure; reduced nuclear arsenals; inhibited the spread of nuclear, biological, and chemical technology and weapons development; and kept outer space free of weapons of mass destruction. Any policy that abrogates these treaties will not enhance national security, but severely jeopardize it.

The adherents of national missile defense might object that we have not yet reached a world of such interdependence, and that, meanwhile, the world is still dangerous. It is, indeed. In this world, military force must still be an option to deter those who would use force, rather than cooperation, and undermine this growing and still fragile structure of economic interdependencies. Much can be said about how U.S. forces, particularly conventional forces, need to be reorganized to help maintain order in a world that is no longer dominated by the Cold War, and how the United States could facilitate the internationalization of force, rather than cling to its unilateral options.

One of the positive effects of globalization is that, in and of itself, it may constitute a deterrent to the use of military force. With economic units no longer confined to national borders, national aggression may well be destructive of such diffused interests, and thereby be considered self-destructive.

Defense also has its limits. While adherents of national missile defense speak of achieving independence of action, it is a policy chimera. Since there will never be absolute confidence in ballistic missile defenses, such defense cannot give the United States freedom of action in a conflict with a developing nation that possesses nuclear-armed ballistic missiles. As we will see in Chapters Five and Six, a fully reliable system providing total security is not possible, not because the technology has not been developed, but because the laws of physics militate against such a system. The question will always remain: Is the United States, or its allies, willing to absorb even a limited number of nuclear detonations on its territory? Freedom of action must always be qualified by the answer to that question.

Consider, for example, the case of the Gulf War had Iraq possessed a few intercontinental ballistic missiles armed with nuclear weapons. Even if the United States had achieved limited missile defense capability, would any American president have led a United Nations coalition in an actual attack of Iraq? Would the free flow of oil to the Western world be considered worth the possible destruction of a major U.S. city? Whatever the answer, the decision to take such a risk would not have been politically possible. Thus, while anti-missile defenses might offer some protection against missile attacks during a crisis situation, they would not allow the United States the freedom of action that its proponents seek.

## THE ROOTS OF AMERICAN UNILATERALISM

Despite limits noted above, proponents of American unilateralism hold to a belief that has its origins in the nation's earliest history. Part of its emotional appeal owes more to long-standing national beliefs than to a sober assessment of reality.

An illustration of this appeal can be found in the rhetoric of former Secretary of State Madeleine Albright. During a recent crisis with Iraq, Albright was asked why the United States could find few friends who agreed with it. It was because, she replied, "we are America, we are the indispensable nation, we stand tall—we see further into the future." Madeleine Albright's view of America as somehow morally different than other countries, not even just superior but out of their league altogether, is a widespread one. So, too, is the tendency of the United States to demonize its enemies, so that a Saddam Hussein or

North Korea's Kim Jong-Il can be portrayed as operating without moral or even rational constraints, as the leaders of "rogue states."

What are the roots of these tendencies? If we go back to the Puritan leader John Winthrop, and the founding of the Massachusetts Bay Colony, we see a people believing that they were establishing a new society in a virgin, unpolluted land as an example of purity before the eyes of God. Their colony was a "city upon a hill," "an example to the nations," free of all the ancient evils of the Old World. Despite the Native American population, they thought themselves alone in the wilderness, cultivating their unique brand of purity. Their society must be kept invulnerable to attack, and, at the same time, it must make its own way, uncompromised by involvement with other societies or countries lacking its purity and mission. Rather than simply being one among many nations, the new society was to be a beacon for other, less enlightened states. By contrast, foreign rulers who oppose it may then easily be characterized as devils who inhabit a degenerate world the colonists left behind.

This way of thinking, initiated in the early seventeenth century, became ingrained in the colonists' foreign policy as they reached nationhood. George Washington, in his farewell address, called upon his countrymen to "steer clear of permanent alliances" ["entangling alliances" was Jefferson's phrase] with any portion of the foreign world." This policy was not isolationism. As the historian Arthur M. Schlesinger, Jr., points out, America "has never been isolationist with regard to commerce. American merchant vessels roamed the seven seas from the first days of independence. Nor has it been isolationist with regard to culture. Its explorers, missionaries, writers, artists, scholars and tourists have ever wandered eagerly about the planet. But through most of its history, America has been stubbornly unilateralist in foreign relations."

Despite the danger that America might face a hostile, united Europe, no such danger appeared until World War I. Through the Monroe Doctrine, with the help of the British fleet, the United States was able to keep Europe from intervening in the affairs of the Western Hemisphere. Major U.S. dealings with foreign powers, such as the purchase of Louisiana or the Mexican-American War, were concerned with the new nation's securing control and possession of what came to be its full territory, rather than becoming one among the world powers.

Eventually worried by German operations in the North Atlantic that threatened its commerce, the United States entered the Great War, but when, at its successful conclusion, Woodrow Wilson attempted to have the United States join the League of Nations, he failed. Wilson's aim was to replace war and an explosive balance of power with a world community that would collectively guarantee the peace. What killed the League in the U.S. Senate was the conflict between the League's power to send American forces into hostilities at its behest and the Constitution's granting of that exclusive power to Congress. Why, the senatorial opposition asked, should Americans die in conflicts where they had no interest, and at the command of others—a question senators have asked recently in connection with American participation in U.N. peacekeeping operations. The League also foundered because of Wilson's arrogant and inept handling of the Senate, a lesson that should have been learned by President Clinton in his mishandling of the Comprehensive Test Ban Treaty. Despite the United States refusal to join, the League of Nations did become the world's major forum, and, of course, the forerunner of the United Nations.

With participation in the League of Nations defeated in the Senate, the United States entered still another period of unilateralism—indeed, in this case, virtual isolationism—in the 1920s and early 1930s. This policy was exemplified by the refusal to join the Permanent Court of International Justice; passage of a forbiddingly high protective tariff; refusal to even discuss collective measures for meeting the world's economic crisis; and rigid neutrality legislation, which made it impossible for the United States to discriminate between aggressors and victims as fascism advanced in Europe.

Franklin Roosevelt, an internationalist, led the country into World War II. Even before the war was over, while internationalism still seemed part and parcel of U.S. wartime coalitions, Roosevelt fostered American participation in such international institutions as the United Nations, the World Bank, and the International Monetary Fund, which seemed to rule out the isolationist politics of the period between the wars. After his death, the Truman Doctrine, the Marshall Plan, NATO, and other security pacts, in Arthur Schlesinger, Jr.'s words, "bound the United States to the outside world in a way that isolationists, in their most pessimistic moments, could hardly have envisaged."

Even in this period, however, unilateralism partially prevailed. The United States, for example, acted with impunity in Central America, just as the French acted in Africa, and the Soviets in Eastern Europe and Afghanistan. Any action that the United States wished to undertake in areas of its hegemony, such as the 1961 invasion at the Bay of Pigs in Cuba or sponsorship of the *contras* in Nicaragua, could be justified as defensive, in view of the Cold War.

President Reagan's original vision of "Star Wars" carried all the hallmarks of American unilateralism. It was a "dream" by which the United States, through its special powers, would be a beacon to the nations of the world by rendering nuclear weapons "impotent and obsolete," and so would end the threat of the evil of nuclear apocalypse that haunted the world. In this thinking, the Soviets were the devils, or people of darkness, represented today by the Saddam Husseins.

Once the Soviet Union collapsed in 1989–1990, however, so did some of the impetus toward internationalism, and the forces for unilateralism reasserted themselves across the whole spectrum of American foreign policy. Today, while the United States still maintains its international involvements, it is increasingly assertive about its position. As the world's dominant political, economic, and military power, America feels it is in a position to insist that other nations do what it tells them, an attitude that surfaces at the United Nations, the International Monetary Fund, and other international bodies. It is manifested when the United States continues its embargoes on Cuba and Iran, and insists on the continuance of the international embargo on Iraq; when it bombs Sudan; when it infiltrates the UN inspection team in Iraq; and when it manifests its willingness to sack the arms control regime and barricade itself behind a wall of national missile defense.

In 1994, with the Republican capture of Congress, Speaker of the House Newt Gingrich signaled the new attack on multilateralism when he accused President Clinton of nurturing a "multilateral fantasy" and a desire "to subordinate the United States to the United Nations." Attacks on the United Nations followed, including refusals to pay regular and peacekeeping assessments, as the Republican majority exercised increasing control of foreign policy. What was lost was the fact that deficiencies of the United Nations would best be cured by engagement, not by the withholding of funds.

Today, unilateralists find themselves in the contradictory position of proposing that the United States exercise global leadership, and, at the same time, withdraw from it. Nowhere is this contradiction more apparent than in the unilateralists' insistence that the United States withdraw from international organizations, treaties, and conventions.[1] What they fail to consider, however, is that these instruments not only inhibit action, they also provide a basis for active cooperation.

Many conservative experts believe they can pick and choose among treaties. Strategic Arms Reduction Treaties are no longer necessary, in their view. The United States does not negotiate with the British and the French on force levels; why should it negotiate with the Russians? The Comprehensive Test Ban and Anti-Ballistic Missile treaties should be jettisoned because they restrain U.S. nuclear weapons development and force options, although there has been little change in the basic design of nuclear weapons in more than twenty years. The Non-Proliferation Treaty, on the other hand, can restrain other nations and should be kept in place, as long as no one takes its Article IV commitment to eventual nuclear disarmament seriously. Better still are export restraint agreements such as the Missile Technology Control Regime and the Australia Group, agreements among the nuclear weapons states to keep technology out of the hands of "states of concern."

But such an *à la carte* treatment fails, as the arms control regime only works as an integrated whole. Without the Comprehensive Test Ban Treaty and serious reduction in U.S. and Russian arsenals, the Non-Proliferation Treaty will lose credibility, as it already has in the case of India and Pakistan, suffering a death by disinterest if not outright defection. Proliferation of missile defenses will undoubtedly weaken the Missile Technology Control Regime, and encourage the proliferation of missiles and defense countermeasures. For those nations without nuclear production capabilities, chemical and biological weapons will hold new appeal. As legal, diplomatic, and political deterrents weaken, it will become easier for nations to shatter the barriers barring their use, possibly triggering a global crisis.

## UNILATERALISM AND THE MILITARY OPTION

One corollary of unilateralism is unnecessary dependence on military solutions. Other solutions, such as arms control agreements, cooperative arrangements to maintain the environment; economic or military aid, and diplomatic efforts to end regional tensions, require the participation and cooperation of other countries. But as the

United States has achieved military hegemony, and maintained its defense establishment at virtual Cold War levels, it increasingly can act alone. Unilateralism and militarization of foreign policy then merge—particularly, as pointed out in the last chapter, when other options are not considered and are underfunded.

The roots of the militarization of U.S. foreign policy lie in the year 1947, with the beginning of the Cold War. In that year, passage of the National Security Act made the armed forces an inherent part of national security policy in peacetime. Previously, the Pentagon had rarely asserted itself in policy formation, even in wartime. Military influence grew over the next four decades, leading to the Goldwater-Nichols Act of 1986, otherwise termed the Defense Reorganization Act, which made the chairman of the Joint Chiefs of Staff the "principal military advisor to the President, the National Security Council, and the Secretary of Defense." As unilateralism reasserted itself, its proponents saw military power as the vehicle through which to exercise their world view.

One of the victims of such politically sponsored militarization has been U.S. adherence to evolving international conventions. In 1999, the United States joined Algeria, China, Libya, Iran, Iraq, and Sudan—ironically, the "rogue states"—in opposing the International Criminal Court (ICC), a body which would extend the scope of international law and provide a means of bringing the world's worst human rights violators to justice. Every member state of the European Union, including America's NATO allies, favors the ICC. Clinton initially pushed the ICC, but he deferred to the Pentagon and Senator Jesse Helms, who resisted exposing American soldiers to international justice. This was a false issue because member nations have the right to try citizens charged with international crimes in their own courts, which is exactly what the United States has done in the past when U.S. soldiers have been involved in criminal activity. The International Criminal Court will be established regardless of the U.S. position, but in a weakened form. Here a major step will be taken in international law without the endorsement of the United States, which pioneered such a move with its support of the Nuremberg trials.

The United States has also been out of step with the global effort to ban the use of land mines, an effort political conservatives and the Pentagon have opposed because of U.S. deployment of such mines near the border between North and South Korea. Although antipersonnel mines have killed and maimed thousands of civilians, including children, all over the world—in Angola, Afghanistan, Bosnia, Cambodia, El Salvador, Mozambique, and elsewhere—the marginal advantage of their deployment in Korea has been the reason justifying U.S. refusal to adhere to the convention. Not even the outbreak of warmer relations between the two Koreas has led to a new position on this issue.

Perhaps a low point for the Clinton administration took place in 1999, when the United States voted against UN efforts to ban the widespread use of soldiers under the age of 18. Nearly 200 nations voted in favor of the ban. Only Somalia, which for all practical purposes had no government, joined the United States in voting no. Only in July 2000, after six years of Pentagon opposition to the ban on child soldiers, did Clinton finally decide to back the ban, which may have been the harbinger of his *volte-face* on National Missile Defense. The Pentagon's opposition was particularly irrational in view of the fact that fewer than 3,000 of the 1.4 million Americans in uniform were under the age of 18 in 2000.

As for the Comprehensive Test Ban Treaty, the Pentagon, weapons laboratories, and conservatives have fought restraints on nuclear weapons testing for four decades, beginning with opposition to the 1963 Partial Test Ban Treaty. As the forces of unilateralism have gained greater control, they have been able to stop the United States from joining virtually the entire rest of the world in limiting nuclear arms. Ratification of the Test Ban would be a major step in preventing nuclear proliferation.

The war in Kosovo was still another exercise in military unilateralism. Even if military force was necessary, and it may well have been, the failure to fully pursue diplomatic solutions and the total reliance on airpower by the United States led to criticism of U.S. actions by its European allies, and eventually to their decision to create their own rapid reaction force. France and Germany had particularly objected to America's strategic bombing of Serbia, involving destruction of bridges across the Danube and unnecessary damage to Serbia's economic infrastructure.

These assertions of military policy, and the retreat from multilateral conventions and organizations, are a throwback to the mechanisms of nineteenth-century imperialism, not the tools of a nation entering the twenty-first century. Militant unilateralism today seems not only destructive, but out of date in a world in which the evolving reality is not sovereign states protected by borders and military forces, but an interconnected world economy regulated by a variety of overlapping jurisdictions.

## THE AMERICAN ROMANCE WITH TECHNOLOGY

National missile defense is not only a unilateralist policy, but one that implies a technical solution to a political problem. Like unilateralism, the American penchant for technological solutions has deep roots in the country's history. Because of this history, Americans believe, with some reason, that technology can solve their problems. They lack justification, however, when they believe that technology can solve *all* of them.

In his "Star Wars" speech of 1983, Ronald Reagan called "upon the scientific community in our country, those who gave us nuclear weapons, to turn their great talents now to the cause of mankind and world peace, to give us the means of rendering these nuclear weapons impotent and obsolete." Not only would these new "smiths of the gods" be able to reverse the evil work they had done, but in so doing, America would once again be a beacon to humankind. Frances Fitzgerald, in *Way Out There in the Blue*, describes a visit Reagan made to the North American Aerospace Defense Command (NORAD) on Cheyenne Mountain, Colorado. She evokes the mythology of technology and spiritual redemption that formed the background of Reagan's 1983 speech:

> Led into the "granite core" of a mountain—into the innermost sanctum of esoteric knowledge—he looks for the first time upon the horror that scientists and their masters have created for the country and for humankind. But then, rather than to accept initiation into the guardianship of this horror, as his predecessors have done, Reagan cuts through the arcane and dangerous knowledge with pure common sense and vows to deliver his people from impending doom.

It was, of course, a thrilling prospect—one that relied on technology, as had the atomic bomb, which it was designed to counter. However, in this case, technology proved unable to provide the desired solution. After Reagan's speech, the idea of a population defense against Soviet missiles through an anti-missile defense system was ridiculed by most technical experts, but as Reagan persevered, the public discounted the experts and believed their president. Fitzgerald writes, "To listen to radio call-shows in 1985 was to hear people from all over the country assailing the experts with arguments such as: people said Alexander Graham Bell was crazy, people said we couldn't get to the moon, now you're telling us scientists can't give us defenses! Nothing in this country is impossible! When experts insisted that science was not magic and that American technology could not do everything, they would be accused of lack of patriotism." Officials in Reagan's administration fell in with this line of thought as a sure way of selling the program, equating confidence in American technical prowess with faith in our country.

What is it about Americans that gives them such faith in technology, sufficient to enable them to "go on faith" with a technological solution to a problem that has thus far proved unsolvable?

Again, one answer lies in history. The early settlers of the colonies that became the United States brought the traditional technologies of their villages, usually in England, with them. But the novel conditions of the New World, and perhaps more importantly, the freedom from the conformity to guilds, labor laws, class codes, government monopolies, and other restrictions, which so dominated the social order in Europe, liberated the colonists to see novel solutions to new problems—to become innovators, not just transmitters, of technology.

The colonies also achieved their independence just at the outbreak of the industrial revolution toward the end of the eighteenth century, when technical progress was flooding Europe. Within one or two generations, manufacturing went from the cottage to the factory, transportation from the coach to the railroad, and power from animals to steam engines. Each basic invention spurred hundreds of sub-inventions, as they spread throughout the economy. While, for Europe, the industrial revolution was simply one phase of its long history, for America it *was* its national history, and so colored Americans' view of what all historical time must look like.

At the beginning of World War I, the United States was still a debtor nation, owing billions of dollars to European banks that had helped finance its industrial growth. By the end of the war, the world's financial center had switched from London to New York, and the nation had moved from debtor to creditor status. America maintained financial leadership in no small part by wave after wave of invention, from the light bulb and telephone to the microchip and computers. One has only to read a book like Ray Kurzweil's *The Age of Spiritual Machines*, with its sure projection of alternative digital realities and sensitive nanorobotic organisms, to see why anything seems technologically possible today. While Kurzweil's specifics are new, his boundless optimism and faith in technology are not. Each generation believes that American technology will totally transform the world, that the sky's the limit—or is it outer space, or is it the furthest reaches of the galaxies?

One problem is that an unqualified faith in technology flies in the face of history. During the European Enlightenment of the eighteenth century, philosophers, such as Denis Diderot, had predicted that technology would eliminate world poverty. The condition of today's world hardly supports that optimism. Fully half the world's population continues to live in dire circumstances, by any conceivable standard, and that half is becoming poorer, relative to the Western industrial countries, year by year.

But even conditions in advanced countries are radically different than those predicted. In the 1950s, for example, Americans believed that if enough money were spent on research, cancer would be cured within a couple of years. It is now 2001, and billions of dollars later, we are still decades away from a basic cure, despite improved treatment methods. Other problems, such as useable nuclear fusion and ion propulsion in space travel, while theoretically feasible, have resisted invention. As John Rennie, editor-in-chief of *Scientific American*, wrote in the magazine's special issue, *Key Technologies for the 21st Century*:

> Films promised that the twilight of the 20th century and the dawn of the 21st would be an era of helpful robot servants, flying jet cars, moon colonies, easy space travel, undersea cities, wrist videophones, paper clothes, disease-free lives and, oh, yes, the 20-hour work week. What went wrong?

> Few of the promised technologies failed for lack of interest. Nor was it the case that they were based on erroneous principles, like the perpetual motion machines that vex patent offices. Quite often, these inventions seemed to work. So why do bad things happen to good technologies? Why do some innovations fall so far short of what is expected of them, whereas others succeed brilliantly?

American "know-how" often works, but the problem, as Rennie explains, is that researchers often fail to see all the complications of their project, and give unrealistically short prospects for their success. Also some ideas contain basic scientific flaws that prevent their realization. Jetpacks, for example, while startling in a James Bond film, didn't work because, it turned out, the fuel would be too heavy. Other technological innovations fail not because they don't work, but for social, political, or economic reasons. For example, the lack of an efficient mass transit system in most American cities is not due to lack of technology, but to a failure of the political system to deliver.

As critics of Edward Teller's "Star Wars" scheme have pointed out, scientists frequently fail to predict all the problems that the engineers who implement their schemes must actually solve. In the case of National Missile Defense, one problem that has proven intractable is the fact that it is far cheaper to put up decoys than to shoot them down, or to discriminate between decoys and nuclear payloads. While it is theoretically possible to shoot them all down—decoys and nuclear payloads—can it be done in the short time a defense system has to do it, and at a cost that makes sense? Faith in technology, in "what made America great," is not enough.

Ironically, the same misguided faith in technology that distorts predictions of success in the development of U.S. anti-missile defense fuels predictions of how fast our opponents can produce effective international ballistic missiles. As we will see in the following chapter, the possibility that "rogue states" such as North Korea or Iran could produce weapons capable of reaching the United States became, in the Rumsfeld report, virtual certainties achievable in the least possible theoretical length of time. The fact that a North Korean missile could theoretically be built in five years meant that it *would* be, despite major technological problems and impeding diplomatic moves. Here, Americans have projected their own unbounded faith and ability in technology onto their enemies.

## LOOKING BACKWARD AND FORWARD

As the United States enters the twenty-first century, it is important that we know our own history but not be tied to it. If we have maintained a unilateralist position in the past, this does not mean we need to do so in the future. If we have had an unbounded and sometimes unfounded faith in technology, we need not continue to do so, but rather understand that technology has its limits, and frequently involves high costs and dangers. As indicated in the Introduction, the world is a vastly different place than it was one hundred years ago. Foreign policy, including our use of force and our deployment of defense resources, needs to become part of this new age, rather than looking backward to an age of self-contained sovereign states.

This is not an abstract debate. If the United States insists on disassembling diplomatic restraints, shattering carefully crafted threat reduction arrangements, and moving from its role of builder to destroyer of the nuclear nonproliferation regime, there will be little to prevent other nations from concluding that their own national security requires nuclear arms. Not only can such a situation result in dangerous conflicts, but nuclear insecurities and regional tensions could freeze foreign investments, strangling economic growth both regionally and globally.

The first two years of George W. Bush's administration will be critical to determining which side in this debate will dominate U.S. policy. U.S. national resources should go into building the world of the future, and its armed forces into maintaining conditions to enable the world to achieve a transition to that world—a peaceful and interdependent global economy.

### NOTE

1. The provisions of the Helms-Biden agreement for payment of our arrears to the United Nations spell out the unilateralist position with remarkable clarity. The agreement demands that no actions be taken by the United Nations or its specialized or affiliated organizations (1) "that require the United States to violate the US Constitution or any laws of the United States"; and (2) that can be interpreted as "exercising sovereignty over the US or taking steps to require the US to cede sovereignty"; (3) that impose a tax or fee "on any United States national"; or (4) that "develop, create, or establish any special agreement under Article 43 of the United Nations Charter to make available to the United Nations, on its call, the armed forces, of any member of the United Nations." One provision even requires certification that the United Nations will not exercise "authority or control over any United States national park" or wildlife preserve.

## RESOURCES

The relationship between the present period and pre-Westphalia Europe is spelled out by Stephen J. Kobrin of the University of Pennsylvania in his brilliant article, "Back to the Future: Neomedievalism and the Postmodern Digital World Economy," in the *Journal of International Affairs* 51, no. 2 (Spring 1998). A recent publication of the Royal Institute of International Affairs (2000), *Understanding Unilateralism in American Foreign Relations*, edited by Gwyn Prins, contains valuable essays that assess American unilateralism in the contemporary world. See particularly Arthur M. Schlesinger, Jr.'s essay, "Unilateralism in Historical Perspective."

An excellent discussion of whether the United States should use its post–Cold War hegemony to "go-it-alone" is given by Robert W. Tucker in "Alone or with Others: The Temptations of Post–Cold War Power," *Foreign Affairs*, November/December 1999.

A fine discussion of the scale of globalization and its implications can be found in Felix Rohatyn's still-relevant articles, "On the Brink," in the June 11, 1987, edition of *The New York Review of Books*, and "America's Economic Dependence," *Foreign Affairs*, Winter 1989. Also important is Peter F. Drucker's *The New Realities* (Harper & Row, 1989), and his article "Multinationals and Developing Countries: Myths and Realities," *Foreign Affairs*, October 1974.

For the conservative point of view, see Paul Wolfowitz, "Bridging Centuries: Fin de Siècle All Over Again," *National Interest*, Spring 1997; Samuel P. Huntington, "The Clash of Civilizations," *Foreign Affairs*, Summer 1993; and James Webb, "Warily Watching China," *New York Times*, February 23, 1999, p. 23. See also Condoleezza Rice, "Promoting the National Interest," *Foreign Affairs*, January/February 2000; the *New York Times* of January 12, 2001, for the view of Donald Rumsfeld, and the *New York Times* of October 25, 1999, for the op-ed of William Kristol and Robert Kagan.

Daniel J. Boorstin's *The Americans: The Colonial Experience* (Random House, 1958) is a splendid introduction to the early history of the country. The other two volumes in his series, *The National Experience* (1965) and *The Democratic Experience* (1973), are also useful for describing the evolving American ethos. Again, Frances Fitzgerald's *Way Out There in the Blue: Reagan, Star Wars and the End of the Cold War* (Simon & Schuster, 2000) has provided excellent background.

For a good coverage of predicted technological developments, see *Key Technologies for the 21st Century: Scientific American: A Special Issue* (W. H. Freeman and Company, 1996). See also Ray Kurzweil, *The Age of Spiritual Machines: When Computers Exceed Human Intelligence* (Viking, 1999); and *Nature's Imagination: The Frontiers of Scientific Vision*, edited by John Cornwell (Oxford University Press, 1995).

For a useful analysis of world conditions and evolving long-term solutions, see *The State of the World: A Worldwatch Institute Report on Progress Toward a Sustainable Society*, edited by Lester R. Brown, Christopher Flavin, and Hilary French (W. W. Norton & Company, 1999 and 2000).

For insight into the militarization of foreign policy, see Dana Priest's excellent three-part series, "A Four-Star Foreign Policy?" in the *Washington Post*, September 28–30, 2000.

# PART II

# THE THREAT, AND EFFORTS TO MEET IT

## Chapter Four

# The Exaggerated Threat of Ballistic Missiles

National missile defense has been pushed to meet the assessment of a threat that goes considerably beyond reality. Forces pushing this threat have been outlined in Part I. In this chapter, we describe just what that assessment has been, how it has been distorted, and what effect it has had on the political campaign to create NMD.

In 1998, the Commission to Assess the Ballistic Missile Threat to the United States, chaired by Donald Rumsfeld, made headlines with its dire warning that North Korea, Iran, and Iraq could deploy an operational intercontinental ballistic missile (ICBM) with "little or no warning." It had become common wisdom, and the official view, that the threat of the United States being attacked by such weapons from "rogue states" was imminent and rising. This perception certainly added to the momentum for the deployment of Clinton's proposed National Missile Defense system and even more expanded schemes. Yet this view was overly influenced by a series of climactic events in 1998, which led to an incomplete and distorted assessment of the threat.

A more balanced net assessment of global ballistic missile arsenals over the past fifteen years would reveal that the threat is confined, limited, and changing relatively slowly. Though the threat to the United States should not be ignored, it does not justify the rush to deployment of national missile defense systems.

1998 was a watershed year that profoundly shaped the perception that missile and nuclear threats to the United States had intensified, and that Americans were living in an increasingly dangerous world. In May 1998, India and Pakistan each tested nuclear weapons. In June, the United States began focusing on the alleged construction of a secret nuclear facility in North Korea. In July, the Rumsfeld Commission released its *Report of the Commission to Assess the Ballistic Missile Threat to the United States*, and Iran tested its Shahab-3 Medium Range Ballistic Missile. In August, thirteen days after terrorists linked to Osama bin Laden attacked U.S. embassies in East Africa, U.S. Tomahawk missiles struck and destroyed one of the world's most prominent terrorist training camps in Afghanistan and a pharmaceutical plant in Khartoum, Sudan. The plant was allegedly producing a chemical used to manufacture nerve gas. Both locations were linked to Osama bin Laden, who, just one day before the strikes, had publicly announced that more Americans would be targeted for murder. Also that month, North Korea launched the Taepo-Dong-1 missile, and the Cox Commission submitted its report to the executive branch on China's alleged thefts of nuclear secrets from U.S. weapons laboratories. Finally, in December, President Clinton ordered U.S. armed forces to strike military and security targets in Iraq in order to "attack Iraq's nuclear, chemical, and biological programs, and its military capacity to threaten its neighbors."

The official view that the missile threat is increasing was greatly influenced by the perception of these events, especially North Korea's missile program and North Korea's willingness to export its missile technology. In the August test launch, the Taepo-Dong-1 flew only 1,320 kilometers, but its international impact was enormous. In 1999, Secretary of Defense William Cohen concluded:

> The Taepo-Dong-1 test was another strong indicator that the United States will, in fact, face a rogue nation missile threat to our homeland against which we will have to defend the American people. Our deployment readiness program has had two key criteria that had to be satisfied before we could make a decision to deploy a limited national missile defense system. There must be a threat to warrant the deployment and our NMD development must have proceeded sufficiently so that we are technologically able to proceed. What we are saying today is that we now expect the first criterion will soon be met, and technological readiness will be the primary remaining criterion.

Within the executive branch, major threat assessment comes from National Intelligence Estimates (NIEs)—documents produced by the National Intelligence Council, whose members are drawn from the CIA and from other agencies that make up the U.S. intelligence community. The 1999 NIE on the ballistic missile threat concluded that, over the next fifteen years, the United States "most likely will face ICBM threats from Russia, China and North Korea, probably from Iran, and possibly from Iraq, although the threats will consist of dramatically fewer weapons than today because of significant reductions we expect in Russian strategic forces." This conclusion was essentially reiterated by the 2000 NIE. Specifically, the reports found that:

> If it had an operable third stage and a reentry vehicle capable of surviving ICBM flight, a converted Taepo-Dong-1 SLV [Space Launch Vehicle] could deliver a light payload to the United States. In these cases, about two-thirds of the payload mass would be required for the reentry vehicle structure. The remaining mass is probably too light for an early generation nuclear weapon but could deliver biological or chemical warfare (BW/CW) agents.

> Most analysts believe that North Korea probably will test a Taepo-Dong-2 this year, unless delayed for political reasons. A two-stage Taepo-Dong-2 could deliver a several-hundred kilogram payload to Alaska and Hawaii, and a lighter payload to the western half of the United States. A three-stage Taepo-Dong-2 could deliver a several-hundred kilogram payload anywhere in the United States.

Iran's 1,300-kilometer Shahab-3 missile, tested in 1998, is allegedly based on the North Korean Nodong, and there is concern that, with North Korean and Russian assistance, Iran could develop a longer-range missile similar to the Taepo-Dong-2.

The assessment projects forward some current technological and development trends. However, by assessing "projected possible and likely missile developments by 2015 independent of significant political and economic changes," it may overestimate potential ballistic missile threats from still developing countries such as Iraq, Iran, and North Korea; underestimate the dangers from existing arsenals in Russia and China; and poorly prepare policy makers for the sharply deteriorated international security environment that would emerge should the nonproliferation regime weaken or collapse.

The unclassified version of the 1999 National Intelligence Estimate reflects a lowering of previously established intelligence agency standards for judging threats. It thus presents known missile programs as more immediate threats than did previous assessments, but this is more a function of the change in three evaluative criteria than of actual change in other nations' missile capabilities:

1. The 1999 NIE concentrated almost exclusively on the possible threat from North Korea, Iran, and Iraq and emphasized who "could" test a long-range missile over the next five to ten years. This is a shift from the previously established standard of when a country "would" deploy a long-range missile. This reflects a shift to a series of worst-case assumptions, independent of significant political and economic changes.

   Conflict within the intelligence community over this shift is evidenced by the inclusion in the NIE of an unusual dissenting opinion from one of the intelligence agencies involved in producing the consensus report: "Some analysts believe that the prominence given to missiles countries 'could' develop gives more credence than is warranted to developments that may prove implausible."

   Official statements on the threat have compounded the damage by interpreting the "could" possibilities as definitive certainties. Secretary Cohen said in March 2000, "The threat is here today. If it's not here right now it will be here tomorrow."

2. The shift in standards from when a country would *deploy* a long-range missile to when a country would *test* a long-range missile represents a difference of five years (i.e., what previous estimates had said was the difference between first test and likely deployment). "With shorter flight test programs—perhaps only one test—and potentially simple deployment schemes," the NIE concludes, "the time between the initial flight test and the availability of a missile for military use is likely to be shortened." This reduction of the test program, of course, would carry the implication of less reliability in the deployed weapon. The Indian experience with the Agni missile provides some indication that the original standard may be the more accurate one. The Agni program began in the mid-1980s. An Agni-1 missile was flight-tested in February 1994, and a medium-range, 2,000-kilometer version, the Agni-2, was tested in April 1999. Despite Indian declarations of intent to deploy, and substantial financial and scientific resources devoted to the program, the missile has yet to enter production.

3. In addition, the previous standard had been to estimate the time it would take to threaten the 48 continental states with a ballistic mis-

sile. The 1999 NIE estimates the threats to any part of the 50 states. The shift of potential U.S. targets represents a range change of some 5,000 kilometers (the distance from Seattle to the western-most tip of the Aleutian Island chain in Alaska). It essentially means that an intermediate-range ballistic missile, such as the Taepo-Dong-1, would be considered the same threat as an intercontinental-range missile. The Taepo-Dong-1 tested on August 31, 1998, impacted 1,320 kilometers from its launch point, and tried but failed to put a small satellite into orbit. This missile does not have the range to strike any part of the United States with a large payload (for example, a nuclear warhead), though it might be able to strike the westernmost parts of Alaska and Hawaii with a very small payload. The Taepo-Dong-2 is theoretically judged to have a range of 4,000 to 6,000 kilometers, allowing it to strike parts of Alaska and Hawaii. A three-stage Taepo-Dong-2 could have a longer range.

Although there is reason to be concerned about citizens in Alaska and Hawaii, a threat only to sparsely inhabited areas of those two states cannot carry the same weight as a threat to all fifty states.

These three changes account for almost all of the differences between the 1999 NIE and earlier estimates. Thus, the new estimate, rather than representing some new, dramatic development in the ballistic missile threat, represents a lowering of the standards for judging the threat. The 1999 estimate led some observers to conclude that there had been a significant technological leap forward in Third World missile systems, when, in fact there had been only incremental development in programs well known to analysts for years.

The 1999 NIE has contributed to an exaggerated sense of the missile threat by focusing its assessment only on weapons programs in a few developing nations, whose political evolution will be a determining factor in whether they remain threats to the United States. Focusing on these few countries gives the distorted view that the global ballistic missile threat is growing. In fact, it is shrinking. The threats the United States now faces remain serious, but they are orders of magnitude removed from those confronted during the Cold War.

Let's start with the big guns. The number of intercontinental ballistic missiles with ranges over 5,500 kilometers has decreased dramatically since the height of the Cold War. These are the only missiles that can reach the continental United States from another nation. During the 1980s, the Soviet Union deployed over 9,540 nuclear warheads on 2,318 such long-range missiles. Currently, Russia has fewer than 5,200 missile warheads deployed on 1,100 missiles. This is a 52 percent decrease in the number of missiles capable of striking the territory of the United States, and a 45 percent decrease in the number of nuclear warheads. These decreases are likely to continue over the next ten years if the pace of disarmament is maintained. With or without new treaties, Russia will likely have fewer than 1,000 nuclear warheads on missiles by 2010—perhaps no more than several hundred, depending on political and economic factors. Thus by 2010, there will be a 90 percent to 94 percent decrease in this threat.

China is presently maintaining a force of some twenty intercontinental ballistic missiles. NIEs predict that this force will remain roughly the same size over the next ten years, although military and political developments (such as a decision by the United States to deploy a national missile defense system) could result in significant increases.

Second, the number of deployed intermediate-range ballistic missiles (with ranges of 3,000 to 5,500 kilometers) has also decreased dramatically. President Ronald Reagan negotiated an arms control treaty in 1987 eliminating this entire class of missiles from U.S. and Soviet arsenals. The Soviet Union destroyed 1,846 such weapons, the United States 846. China has some 20 missiles in this range, but no other nation has developed missiles this powerful. Granted, if North Korea perfects its developmental Taepo-Dong-2, this would add a few weapons to this category. Still, there has been close to a 100 percent decrease in the threat posed by intermediate-range missiles.

Third, only six nations have medium-range missiles with a 1,000 to 3,000-kilometer range (Israel, Saudi Arabia, India, Pakistan, North Korea, and Iran). These medium-range ballistic missiles do not threaten the territory of the United States. India intends to begin production of the Agni-2, with a range of about 2,000 kilometers. The North Korean Nodong is the basis for Pakistan's Ghauri and Ghauri II missiles and Iran's Shahab-3, all of which have been flight-tested. Only four of these nations have active programs for trying to stretch the range of these systems to over 3,000 kilometers in the next 10 years (India, Pakistan, North Korea, and Iran).

In addition to the quantitative reduction in ballistic missile arsenals, the number of countries trying or threatening to develop long-range missiles has decreased and changed qualitatively. The nations now attempting to do so are smaller, poorer, and less technologically advanced than were the nations with missile programs fifteen years ago. Missile technology is not spreading rapidly around the globe.

We now worry primarily about five nations, in addition to Russia and China: North Korea, Iran, Iraq, India, and Pakistan. Fifteen years ago, the perceived threat was greatest from India, Brazil, Argentina, Egypt, South Africa, and Libya, all of which were involved in programs to develop long-range missiles. All but India have since terminated their efforts. Israel retains the capability to develop long-range missiles, but is not considered a threat to the United States, nor a likely exporter of missile technology.

Finally, the blurring of short and intercontinental ranges for the world's missile inventory results in a widely held belief in policy circles that twenty-five nations possess ballistic missiles. That is true, but China and Russia are still the only potential adversaries with the capability to hit the United States with nuclear-armed missiles. This has not changed since the Soviet Union and China deployed their first intercontinental ballistic missiles in 1959 and 1981, respectively. Almost all of the nations that possess ballistic missiles have only short-range systems. Specifically, apart from the five recognized nuclear-weapon states, there are thirty-three nations with ballistic missiles, but the vast majority, or twenty-seven nations, have only short-range missiles under 1,000 kilometers. In fact, 22 of the 33 nations only have aging Scuds, which are declining in military utility over time, or similar short-range missiles of 300-kilometer range or less. This confusion is perpetuated when policy makers speak of threats from missiles to the United States or U.S. interests, such as forward-deployed troops or allies. This again merges threats from very short-range missiles, of which there are many, with long-range missiles, of which there are few.

In short, the most accurate way to summarize existing global ballistic missile capabilities is that there is a widespread capability to launch short-range missiles, mostly Scuds. There is a slowly growing, but still limited, capability to launch medium-range missiles. Most importantly, there is a decreasing number of long-range missiles that can threaten the United States.

## NORTH KOREA

It is impossible to deny that North Korea and Iran could eventually pose some ballistic missile threat to the United States. However, the threat posed by these countries is much smaller than presumed by the 1998 Rumsfeld Commission and the 1999 and 2000 NIEs, and in no way justifies a rush to deployment of a national missile defense.

Clearly, the threat posed to the United States by North Korea should not be ignored. North Korea maintains one million men under arms; it is the only nation in the world technically in an active military confrontation with the United States; and it has steadily pursued a program to turn short-range Scud technology into longer-range rockets. In the 1990s, North Korea tested and then deployed a 1,000-kilometer-range missile, the Nodong, based on clustered Scud engines. On August 31, 1998, North Korea tested a Taepo-Dong-1 missile, which is believed to be a Nodong with a Scud-like second stage and a small third stage kick-motor, used in a failed attempt to orbit a small satellite. In addition, North Korea could have acquired enough plutonium to build one or two nuclear weapons, according to CIA reports.

Yet it is important to keep the North Korean threat in perspective. North Korea, after all, is a small nation, intermittently hit with famine, whose population of 21 million is the same as that of Taiwan, but which struggles to produce a $14 billion Gross National Product that is less that 4 percent of Taiwan's. The government spends an estimated $2 billion per year on defense, or about one-half the annual U.S. budget for missile defense programs. North Korea has only tested two longer-range missiles, a number that dwindles in comparison with the large number of tests conducted by Russia and China over the years. In addition, experts have assessed that the threat posed by North Korea's missile program has been exaggerated. In their analysis of the North Korean test facility, the Federation of American Scientists reported:

> The vaunted Nodong test site is a facility barely worthy of note, consisting of the most minimal imaginable test infrastructure. . . . It is quite evident that this facility was not intended to support, and in many respects is incapable of supporting, the extensive test program that would be needed to fully develop a reliable missile system. . . . [T]he most noteworthy features . . . are those that are entirely absent: the transportation links, paved roads, propellant storage, and staff housing that would be needed to support an extensive test program.

Finally, the political conditions and decisions made by the North Korean leadership will profoundly affect the North Korean missile program, and a threat assessment must not ignore positive political developments. In June 2000, North Korean leader Kim Jong Il and South Korea's Kim Dae Jong held a historic first meeting in Pyong-yang. The two leaders agreed on modest steps to improve future relations, including allowing visits between families divided since the Korean War, as well as economic and cultural exchanges. Given the fact that the two sides have only exchanged insults and bullets for years, this has to be considered great progress. The United States responded by lifting some North Korean economic sanctions. The following month, Russian President Putin reported that North Korea offered to give up its missile program in exchange for access to other countries' rockets for space research. Kim Jong Il also agreed to visit Russia. Finally, U.S. Secretary of State Madeleine Albright met with Foreign Minister Paek of the Democratic People's Republic of North Korea in the first bilateral meeting at the ministerial level ever held between the two countries. These recent events are encouraging signs that the North Korean government is coming out of its self-imposed isolation and is acting constructively to improve its international po-sition, including its ability to provide for its population.

Negotiations have worked in the past, including an Agreed Frame-work in 1994 which allowed the investigations of North Korea's Kumchon-Ni facility by Western observers when suspicious activity took place there in 1998.

Despite this impressive record, during his March 7, 2001, meeting with South Korean President Kim Dae Jung, President Bush squan-dered the opportunity to conclude a verifiable, permanent end to North Korea's long-range missile program. He stated that talks started in the Clinton era would not resume soon but only at "some point in the future." This was perhaps risking the best opportunity to defeat potential, long-range North Korean missiles.

Moreover, deterrence has worked well in the past against a North Korean attack, and continues to be a powerful tool on the Korean pen-insula. Few doubt that U.S. military forces on the Korean Peninsula, and the threat of a nuclear retaliation, have effectively prevented a full-scale North Korean attack for half a century. If North Korea's leader-ship is rational, then it can be deterred through traditional methods from attacking the United States with missiles and nuclear weapons. In addition, it is quite possible that continued negotiations between the United States and North Korea could yield a diplomatic resolu-tion, a verifiable agreement to end its missile and nuclear programs.

According to officials in the United States, the North Korean missile program and its testing are the key factors in determining the parameters and the deployment schedule and capabilities of a U.S. national missile defense system. Therefore, a change in the North Korean development program ought to mean a change in the deployment schedule for NMD. Presumably if a test that the intelligence community predicted would take place in 1999 has still not taken place by the end of 2001, the timelines for expected deployment of the U.S. system should shift as well. In addition, it seems foolish to ignore the remarkable political developments on the peninsula that began with the 2000 summit. It would be a great embarrassment and a tragic waste of money if the United States rushed to deploy a $60 billion system in the Pacific, designed to protect against a threat that may well no longer exist.

## IRAN

Iran is also considered a nation aspiring to threaten the United States with ballistic missiles, as, since the early 1970s, it has labored to develop an advanced ballistic missile capability. In July 2000, Iran completed its first successful test of the Shahab-3, a medium-range missile capable of hitting targets in Saudi Arabia, Israel, and Turkey. Even after this test, however, the missile is only available for "emergency operational deployment," according to Iranian officials. Furthermore, the missile has never been tested to its claimed range of 1,300 kilometers, and it is highly inaccurate, with only about a 50 percent chance of landing within four kilometers of its target. Overall, the returns to Iran's substantial investments in developing ballistic missiles have been mediocre. This year's Shahab-3 test came a full twenty-five years after Iran first developed and tested unguided rockets.

Most advancements in Iranian missile capabilities have been driven by external assistance from North Korea, Russia, and China. More importantly, changes in the diplomatic environment could obviate the Iranian threat. For example, as U.S.-Iranian relations continue to warm and the domestic influence of Iranian conservatives wanes, Iranian financial support for missile programs could be cut. Indirectly, successful U.S. efforts to prevent North Korean, Chinese, and Russian missile exports would strangle Iran's program.

Even if Iran could develop a long-range missile capability in the near future, it is not clear that Iranian leaders wish to do so. Iran's priority is not to threaten the U.S. homeland, but to establish regional hegemony by challenging the supremacy of U.S. military forces in the Middle East. For this objective, intercontinental ballistic missiles are unnecessary, and the Shahab-3 is inconsequential. In February 1999, Iranian Defense Minister Ali Shamkhani stated that "the Shahab-3 missile is the last military missile Iran will produce. We have no plans for another war missile." Shamkhani insisted that the Shahab-3 would adequately serve Iran's national security needs, and that any further missile development (such as the Shahab-4, a program thought to be based on Russian SS-4 technology) would be directed toward Iran's space launch vehicle program.

In short, Iran's missile capabilities are poor and brittle. A quarter-century of ballistic missile acquisition efforts has not yielded a threat that would justify NMD deployment by the United States. Furthermore, its highly inaccurate missiles pose little threat to U.S. troops stationed in the Middle East, unless equipped with a nuclear warhead, which Iran does not possess.

## IRAQ

Iraq remains under severe United Nations sanctions. Even when these sanctions are eventually lifted, it is highly unlikely that Iraq could develop an ICBM within the next fifteen years. It is very difficult, if not impossible, to leap from short-range Scuds to intercontinental missiles. It is likely that Iraq would first try to develop medium-range missiles that could threaten its neighbors, including Israel and Iran. Under these circumstances, there would be a strong regional response to Iraqi programs that very well could prevent Iraq from proceeding further with its missile programs. It is also very likely that over the next fifteen years there will be a change in the Iraqi regime that could result in the restoration of friendly relations with the United States.

## RUSSIA AND CHINA

In addition to grossly overestimating the missile threats posed by North Korea, Iran, and Iraq, the 1999 NIE underestimates the potential threat posed by Russia and China. The assessment assumes that China and Russia will follow essentially status quo paths. According to the NIE, the Russian threat will continue to be "the most robust and lethal, considerably more so than that posed by China, and orders of magnitude more than that posed by the other three [North Korea, Iran and Iraq]." The report notes that budget constraints will force the Russian government to reduce the number of deployed missiles, and concludes that an unauthorized or accidental launch "is highly unlikely so long as current technical and procedural safeguards are in place." However, there is considerable evidence of major problems with Russian command and control systems. The continuing Russian decline could severely weaken current safeguards and increase the risk of launches because of misjudgment. After it made a similar assessment of the low risk of accidental or unauthorized launch, the previous NIE, performed in 1995, cautioned, "We are less confident about the future, in view of the fluid political situation in both countries [Russia or China]. If there were a severe political crisis in either country, control of the nuclear command structure could become less certain, increasing the possibility of an unauthorized launch."

The 1999 NIE also finds that China will only field a few tens of intercontinental ballistic missiles, its current "minimum deterrent" plan. That, too, could change dramatically if the United States and Japan deploy missile defenses in East Asia. China might well believe it must preserve its nuclear deterrent by increasing the number and sophistication of its missiles. Because Russia and, to a lesser extent, China still pose the greatest potential missile threats to the United States, it is important to consider whether a limited NMD would truly be effective against potential missile launches from those countries.

For some analysts, the real point of national missile defense is not North Korea at all, but China. They believe that a U.S.-China clash is almost inevitable. In order to preserve U.S. freedom of action, these analysts argue that the United States cannot allow any nation to trump its superior military forces with a nuclear-armed missile. In this view, a missile defense is absolutely essential to give a future president the confidence to proceed in a military showdown, certain that the United States could defeat a missile attack.

The Chinese, however, see this from the opposite side. They believe that U.S. missile defenses, particularly in conjunction with Japan, are an offensive move. They call it "the shield followed by the sword." To prevent what they believe would be an effort to coerce China militarily, they would likely expand their nuclear weapons arsenal, building more missiles, equipping some with multiple warheads (compared to the single warhead each now carries), and adding decoys and other countermeasures to defeat missile defenses. A recent test of a new missile included such decoys.

Russia, meanwhile, has announced plans to dramatically reduce its nuclear arsenal from the approximately 6,000 nuclear warheads currently deployed, including those deliverable by plane, to under 1,500 by the end of the decade. But Russian leaders have warned that future reductions are highly conditioned on the United States not deploying a missile defense system. Their logic is similar to the Chinese. If they reduce their arsenal to low levels, a U.S. missile defense might negate what Russia considers its deterrent force, exposing it to nuclear coercion. Russian leaders will strive to keep their arsenal large enough to overwhelm any U.S. defense, even if it entails great national sacrifice. Thus, instead of providing defense, a deployed NMD system could provoke responses from Russia and China that would actually exacerbate the threat.

## OTHER COUNTRIES

Whether more nations acquire more and longer-range missiles also depends fundamentally on the perceived vitality of the international nonproliferation regime. If, for example, the Senate does not reconsider its refusal to ratify the Comprehensive Test Ban Treaty, the treaty cannot enter into force. With the treaty's future highly uncertain, India is unlikely to sign it, and without India, nor will Pakistan. Russian and Chinese ratification of the treaty also becomes unlikely.

Over the next few years, it is highly probable that one or all of these nations would then resume testing of nuclear weapons. A comprehensive test ban freezes the development in those nations having less-developed weapons. The incentive to resume testing is thus greater for China than for Russia, and greatest for India and Pakistan. Faced with a weakened international regime, uncertain U.S. adherence to international commitments, and the emergence of new nuclear nations, Japanese leaders may also believe that they have no choice but to develop their own nuclear deterrent, fundamentally altering the global strategic landscape.

The NIE does not deal with Japan, nor have previous unclassified NIE reports. This is not because Japan is incapable of developing an intercontinental ballistic missile with a nuclear warhead. In fact, Japan could develop an ICBM in a very short time. Indeed, as the 1995 NIE stated: "Three countries not hostile to the United States—India, Israel and Japan—could develop ICBMs within as few as five years if they were motivated, but we judge that they are unlikely to make the necessary investments during the period of this estimate." That is, military capabilities in these countries were evaluated in light of political and economic considerations. Thus, while these countries could develop ICBMs, the intelligence agencies concluded that, in their political judgment, they would not since their primary military interests are regional. However, if the international moratorium on nuclear testing ends, the negotiated nuclear reduction process with Russia collapses, funding is slashed for U.S. programs that help Russia reduce its nuclear stockpiles, missile defenses are deployed in large numbers, or the Non-Proliferation Treaty appears to be an empty promise, India, Israel, Japan, and other nations would likely have strong motivation for developing or accelerating the development of indigenous nuclear weapons and delivery vehicles.

The catastrophic collapse of the nonproliferation regime would have a far more profound influence on the spread of nuclear weapons and advanced long-range missile technology than would the test of an intermediate-range missile in North Korea, even one with the theoretical capability of reaching the continental United States with a small payload. However, while the latter is analyzed in the NIE, the former is not. This results in an incomplete and distorted picture of the influences and constraints on national missile programs.

## FORWARD-BASED THREATS: "THE SUITCASE BOMB ARGUMENT"

The 1999 and 2000 NIEs estimate also contains critical findings that may be overlooked or misused if the reports are viewed solely as a justification for a decision to deploy a national missile defense system. One of the most important findings is included only at the end, namely that there are several other means to deliver weapons of mass destruction to the United States that would be more reliable, less expensive, and more accurate than potential new ICBMs over the next fifteen years.

As previous NIEs have reported (in 1993 and 1995), any new nation seeking to develop an ICBM faces formidable technological obstacles, including but not limited to propulsion technology, guidance and re-entry vehicle technology, and the difficult task of actually construct-ing a lightweight nuclear warhead. Given the difficulties of ICBM development, it is important to consider other delivery systems that emerging proliferators might pursue. The 1999 and 2000 NIEs per-form a significant service by discussing, in greater detail than previous unclassified assessments, the dangers posed by delivery vehicles other than ICBMs, including forward-based launchers (sea-based short- or medium-range ballistic missiles, cruise missiles, and aircraft) and co-vert delivery by ship, plane, or land. The terrorist attack against the billion-dollar destroyer the USS *Cole* in October 2000 dramatically illustrated this danger in a nonnuclear context.

The 1999 NIE notes that these delivery methods, while not as prestigious as ICBMs, are "of significant concern," and "might be the means of choice for terrorists." They offer many attractive advantages over the development of long-range missiles, including that they would be significantly less expensive; they could be covertly developed and deployed; they would be more reliable than ICBMs; they would be more accurate than ICBMs over the next fifteen years; they would be more effective for disseminating a biological or chemical warfare agent than a ballistic missile; and they would negate missile defenses.

Compared to nationally delivered ICBMs, the threat to the United States is probably much greater from nonstate actors, and from non-nuclear weapons with short-range, nonmissile delivery systems. Against such simpler systems, NMD is neither designed nor capable of offering any defense. Robert Walpole, the CIA analyst primarily responsible for producing the NIE, testified before the Senate in Feb-ruary 2000 that nonmissile delivery and nonidentifiable actors are the most likely threat:

> In fact, we project that in the coming years, U.S. territory is probably more likely to be attacked with weapons of mass destruction from non-missile delivery means (most likely from non-state entities) than by missiles, primarily because non-missile delivery means are less costly and more reliable and accurate. They can also be used without attri-bution.

These two observations imply that, to the extent that the missile threat is increasing, NMD may not be viable as a means to protect the United States.

## RESOURCES

The following articles provide a good context for this discussion: "U.S. Plays Down Fear of Rogue Nations," *Chicago Tribune*, February 15, 2000; "Politics Mixes with Strategy in Plan for Antimissile System," *New York Times*, June 23, 2000; and "U.S. Study Reopens Division Over Nuclear Missile Threat," *New York Times*, July 5, 2000.

See National Intelligence Council, "National Intelligence Estimate (NIE): Foreign Missile Development and the Ballistic Missile Threat to the United States Through 2015," unclassified summary, September 1999. This is thoroughly discussed in Andrew M. Sessler (chair of the study group) et al., "Countermeasures: A Technical Evaluation of the Operational Effectiveness of the Planned US National Missile Defense System," a publication of the Union of Concerned Scientists, April 2000, which contains an exhaustive discussion of countermeasures. While for the most part it is written for the general reader, the appendices require more of a technical background. It is available online at *www.ucsusa.org*. Printed copies may be ordered from Publications Department, Union of Concerned Scientists, P.O. Box 9105, Cambridge, MA 02238–9105; by e-mail at *pubs@ucsusa.org*; or by telephoning (617) 547–5552. Chapter Ten of this report gives a general discussion of the testing of military systems and specific requirements and recommendations for the NMD system. See also "Emerging Missile Threats to North America During the Next 15 Years," National Intelligence Community Report NIE-95–19, November 1995.

Further background is provided in "Written Statement for Hearing of the House National Security Committee, 28 February 1996," of Richard N. Cooper, chairman of the National Intelligence Council, titled "Emerging Missile Threats to North America During the Next 15 Years," reprinted in "The Last 15 Minutes: Ballistic Missile Defense in Perspective," edited by Joseph Cirincione and Frank von Hippel, published by The Coalition to Reduce Nuclear Dangers, 21 Dupont Circle NW, Washington, DC 20036. See also Janne Nolan, *An Elusive Consensus: Nuclear Weapons and American Security After the Cold War* (The Brookings Institution, 1999); and Stephen Schwartz, ed., *Atomic Audit* (The Brookings Institution, 1999). See also "National Missile Defense: *What Does It All Mean*? A CDI Issue Brief," Center for Defense Information, September 2000. For access information, see Resources for Chapter One.

Joseph Cirincione's views on the threat issue are to be found in "Assessing the Assessment: The 1999 National Intelligence Estimate of the Ballistic Missile Threat," *The Nonproliferation Review*, Spring 2000.

## Chapter Five

# Why National Missile Defense Won't Work

He thought he saw an Argument
That proved he was the Pope:
He looked again, and found it was
A Bar of Mottled Soap.
"A fact so dread," he faintly said,
"Extinguishes all hope!"

Lewis Carroll, *Sylvie and Bruno*

Wipe your glosses with what you know.

James Joyce

As noted in Chapter One, President Reagan's charge was stunning: "I call upon the scientific community in this country, who gave us nuclear weapons, to turn their great talents to the cause of mankind and world peace; to give us the means of rendering these weapons impotent and obsolete." Secretary of State George Schultz tried to tone the statement down, but failed. In frustration, he blamed, among others, the president's science advisor, George Keyworth, saying, "You are a lunatic." When Schultz first realized that the president's desire for a defense against nuclear weapons was serious and that the president intended to make what became the famous "Star Wars" speech, he told his aides, "We don't have the technology to say this."

And we didn't. Today Schultz would no doubt say the same thing about the proposed National Missile Defense system, the direct descendant of "Star Wars." And it wouldn't matter whether one was talking about President Clinton's version or the far larger system proposed in 2000 by more extreme elements of the Republican party, including the extension proposed by President George W. Bush to protect U.S. allies in Europe, the Middle East, and Asia.

Why Schultz's comment would be the same today can be stated in a single sentence: "The X-band radar, visible, and infrared sensors used by the National Missile Defense system cannot distinguish between real warheads and decoys, nor will an increase in their performance allow them to do so." Easily said, but what does it mean? And how can we be certain? This chapter will attempt to answer these questions.

To begin with, we need to understand about the trajectory of an intercontinental ballistic missile. Almost all of such a missile consists simply of fuel and a motor designed to lift some payload into space, which will then travel without propulsion, and, if properly directed, will drop on the target, following the laws of gravity. The first "stage," which propels the missile, is known as the "booster," and there may be several additional stages that provide propulsion to lift the payload into space.

Rocket boosters may be powered by liquid or solid fuel. Liquid-fueled boosters are complex mechanical devices, while solid-fueled ones are deceptively simple. They are deceptive in that it is quite difficult to master the chemical engineering and fabrication techniques needed for the high-explosive solid fuel to burn uniformly. It also takes a good deal of knowledge of materials science to fabricate the special materials needed for nozzles and for casings that will not burst under the high pressures developed by the motors. This is why most developing countries use liquid-fueled rockets in spite of their complexity and reduced reliability; they are within the capabilities of their countries' industrial base.

The period that the warhead spends in space is known as "midcourse." In the case of a simple intercontinental ballistic missile, there would be a single warhead enclosed in what is known as a re-entry vehicle. The final phase is "re-entry," when the warhead re-enters the atmosphere on the way to its target. So the trajectory of a ballistic missile consists of three phases: powered flight, during which the rocket fuel is burned; free ballistic flight, which corresponds to mid-course; and, finally, its aerodynamic re-entry. Mid-course represents more than 80 percent of the flight time.

Defenses can be designed to attack the missile during its boost phase, or the warhead during mid-course, or at re-entry. Each approach has its own unique virtues and difficulties. The National Missile Defense system proposed by President Clinton is designed to attack the warhead in the near vacuum of space before it re-enters the atmosphere; it is therefore a type of mid-course defense. Interception relies on the high relative velocity between the warhead and a hit-to-kill maneuverable "kill vehicle" designed to strike the warhead dead-on, thereby destroying it by the force of the impact. Given the velocities of the warhead and the kill vehicle (about 8 to 10 kilometers per second), this has appropriately been characterized as trying to hit a bullet with a bullet. While this is, in and of itself, a very difficult task, it may actually be achievable, although not with certainty or even with a high success rate, given current technology. Defensive systems that rely on other means of destroying the ballistic missile than hit-to-kill are discussed in the next chapter.

But a missile need not carry only a single warhead. The payload may also carry lightweight chaff (essentially small pieces of wire or aluminum) and decoys that could confuse the interceptor's sensors. The decoys can be lightweight—a metal-coated mylar balloon is a good example—since once the payload is in the vacuum of space that characterizes the mid-course part of the rocket's trajectory, all its elements—warhead or warheads, decoys, and chaff—travel at the same velocity without any slowing due to atmosphere.

In the case of chemical or biological payloads, which will be discussed later, the warhead can be subdivided into many small bomblets known as submunitions. The proposed defense would be useless against a missile carrying submunitions, as it cannot hit many, separated targets. It is also useless against decoys, as it cannot distinguish them from the warhead.

How does the kill vehicle detect and identify its target? (It is called an "exoatmospheric kill vehicle" (see Figure 1) as it is designed to destroy its target above the atmosphere.) In the case of a single warhead, it can detect infrared and reflected visible light emitted by the payload or re-entry vehicle within which the warhead is enclosed. If the re-entry vehicle is illuminated by radar, it can be detected by the radar's reflected short wavelength radio waves. (The radars for the

Figure 1. Raytheon Exoatmospheric Kill Vehicle. The vehicle is approximately 55 inches long, 23 inches in diameter, and weighs about 121 pounds. The cylindrical object on top is the telescope. Two rocket motors for lateral thrust and associated fuel tanks are readily visible. (Ballistic Missile Defense Organization)

proposed National Missile Defense system use a wavelength of about 3 centimeters, known as X-band.) This information constitutes the vehicle's "signature." The infrared, which is an electromagnetic form of radiation whose wavelength falls between radar and visible light, is emitted by the re-entry vehicle because of its temperature. This is the kind or radiation picked up by night-vision telescopes or goggles.

Unfortunately for the defense system, all of the emissions from the re-entry vehicle that constitute its signature can be mimicked by cheap, lightweight decoys. The number of decoys deployed on each missile could vary between ten and, say, fifty, depending on the sophistication of the design used to reduce their weight and their associated gas bottles and dispensing mechanism.

It might be helpful at this point to understand how the anti-ballistic missile systems proposed during the Cold War dealt with the problem of distinguishing between warheads, decoys, and chaff (collectively known as the "threat cloud"). It was generally accepted in those days that a warhead could not be reliably identified in the threat cloud. These older systems therefore depended on a technique that did not require the system to distinguish between the warheads and decoys in mid-course. Instead, the warhead had to be intercepted *after* it entered the atmosphere; the time available for the intercept was therefore dramatically shortened. This had the consequence of making anti-ballistic missile systems using this approach incapable of offering a reliable defense. Although such a system was deployed around Moscow, U.S. defense planners gave it no weight in their targeting strategy. One reason was that the system was highly vulnerable to countermeasures. In March 1987, Lawrence Woodruff, then deputy undersecretary of defense for strategic and theater nuclear forces, stated to the House Armed Services Committee:

> The Soviets have been developing their Moscow [ABM] defenses for over ten years at a cost of billions of dollars. For much less expense, we believe we can still penetrate these defenses with a small number of Minuteman missiles equipped with highly effective chaff and decoys. And if the Soviet should deploy more advanced or proliferated defenses, we have new penetration aids as counters under development. We are developing a new maneuvering re-entry vehicle that could evade interceptor missiles.

In fact, such a maneuverable re-entry vehicle had already been developed and tested for the navy, but was never deployed because of a lack of necessity. For these reasons, the Joints Chiefs of Staff were always supremely confident of the United States' ability to overwhelm and penetrate the Moscow anti-ballistic missile systems.

In these older systems, once the warheads and decoys were deployed in space by the incoming missile, large phased array radars[1] tracked all the warheads and decoys, and the trajectory of each object was stored in a computer's memory. When the warheads and decoys entered the atmosphere, the warheads could easily be identified, since the lighter decoys would be stripped away by the atmosphere's resistance. Once the warheads were identified, their trajectories could be recalled from all previously stored trajectories, and the aim point for the warheads determined. Information about the trajectory and aim point was then passed to "battle management radars" that would guide the interceptors to the warheads.

Even with nuclear-tipped interceptors it was clear, as early as the 1960s, that, in the words of President Eisenhower's Secretary of State John Foster Dulles, the system would at best "degrade gracefully," meaning that it could be rapidly overwhelmed by the large number of warheads, computational limitations, and the limited time available for intercept. The proposed National Missile Defense system proposed by President Clinton does not rely on the atmosphere to strip away decoys from the incoming warhead, but must perform the very difficult if not impossible task of discriminating between them in the vacuum of space.

In the proposed NMD, the exoatmospheric kill vehicle has a telescope that can observe targets in the visible and at least two infrared wavelengths. Even at the rather close range of ten kilometers, or one second before impact, the telescope's resolution, or size of an object that can be seen distinctly, is only about 1.5 to 3 meters. Thus, the exoatmospheric kill vehicle sees both decoys and warheads, which are smaller than 1.5 meters, as unresolved points of light. The vehicle's sensor signal analysis programs must therefore attempt to find the warhead by examining how each point of light, corresponding to a warhead or decoy, fluctuates in time. The intensity of the signal from each potentially lethal object depends on its size, temperature, surface materials, and spatial orientation; and the fluctuation in the signal from each object depends on how its orientation changes in time. Data from past National Missile Defense tests (see Appendix Two) show that there was no fluctuating feature in the signals from decoys and warheads that could be used to distinguish one object from the other.

This is the bottom line: the problem isn't technology, it's physics. Decoys and warheads can always be made to emit almost identical signals in the visible, infrared, and radar bands; their signatures can be made virtually the same.

Warheads can also be enclosed in a metal-coated balloon or similar device—a concept called "anti-simulation"—to make it appear to the interceptor's sensors to be a decoy. Since, as we have noted, there is no unique signature that can be used to determine which object in the threat cloud is the warhead, no amount of development of the defense sensors or their associated analysis programs will allow discrimination of the warhead from a decoy.

Furthermore, not much can be done to increase the resolution of the telescope because of fundamental limitations imposed by the wavelength one is observing (visible or infrared) and the telescope's diameter, which is constrained by what can fit into the kill vehicle. This means that further research and development cannot make the hit-to-kill technology into a credible basis for a national missile defense. This problem is not new; its solution has eluded the best minds in the business for many, many years.

Of course, one could hope that a country choosing to attack the United States with an intercontinental ballistic missile would for some unfathomable reason not deploy countermeasures. But if that country can develop intercontinental ballistic missiles, it can deploy decoys and chaff. Indeed, the CIA and the U.S. Air Force's National Air Intelligence Center report that, in August of 1999, China tested its road-mobile Dongfeng-31 (DF-31) missile with penetration aids that included decoys and chaff.

China in the past has shown little hesitation in sharing its technology with "states of concern." Indeed, the Air Force report concluded that "Russia and China have each developed numerous countermeasures and probably will sell some related technologies." The 1999 U.S. National Intelligence Estimate dealing with the ballistic missile threat to the United States reached the same conclusion. Besides, as the CIA points out, the making and deploying of countermeasures is technically far simpler than building and deploying intercontinental ballistic missiles with nuclear warheads, and is well within the capability of developing nations that could deploy the missiles. Decoys, chaff, and anti-simulation will be used.

## THE COST OF COUNTERMEASURES

The importance of decoys or submunitions is that they are, in and of themselves, highly effective countermeasures to the planned National Missile Defense system, and would overwhelm any missile defense designed to intercept targets well after boost phase. Defense would require an impossible number of defending missiles for each attacking missile. That is, in Paul Nitze's phrase, the defense is not "cost effective at the margin," as countermeasures cost a small fraction—generally less than one-hundredth—of the cost of the defensive missile needed to knock them out.

In putting together an effective national missile defense system, the designer must worry about vulnerability and cost-effectiveness. To begin with, the proposed system is highly vulnerable because its interceptors and X-band radars are ground-based, and any state choosing to attack the United States with a few intercontinental missiles would make them prime targets for destruction just before the attack.

The issue of cost-effectiveness at the margin depends on how many missiles would be needed to destroy the payload of one attacking missile. Theoretically, if this is more than one, the defense is not cost-effective at the margin. But the ratio of defending to attacking missiles is actually much larger than one; when decoys, which cannot be distinguished from the warhead or warheads, are used, the number of defending missiles becomes enormous, since each object must be targeted. That is why decoys defeat the system, and even a relatively poor country capable of deploying intercontinental missiles can defeat the proposed National Missile Defense system.

On the other hand, even if the warhead can be distinguished from the decoys (and this would take a wonderfully cooperative enemy), it may nonetheless take many interceptors to defend against one attacking missile. Nothing is perfect. So, for example, if the rocket portion of the defending interceptor has a reliability of 90 percent, and the probability of finding the warhead among the decoys is 90 percent, and the chance of hitting the attacking warhead after discrimination is 90 percent (all extremely optimistic numbers), the chance of hitting the warhead with one interceptor is only about 73 percent. Now, with a 73 percent chance of stopping an attacking missile with one interceptor, if one wants a 98 percent chance of stopping the attacking missile, not unreasonable since it presumably carries a nuclear warhead, one would need three interceptors for each attacking missile—not bad, if an attacking country only has a few missiles.

Now let's try somewhat more realistic numbers. If an adversary deploys twenty-four decoys and one warhead, the probability of picking out the warhead in the threat cloud by chance alone is 4 percent. Even though there is no unique signature that can be used to identify the warhead, let us use 20 percent for the probability of discrimination (five times better than it deserves), 80 percent for the rocket, and 80 percent for hitting the warhead (still very optimistic). Then the number of interceptors required for a 90 percent chance of stopping the attacking missile is seventeen; for a 98 percent chance, the number is twenty-nine. In reality, under real-world operational conditions, the probability of a successful intercept could well be far smaller than these estimates—surely not cost effective at the margin![2]

## CHEMICAL AND BIOLOGICAL WEAPONS

Before moving on to other aspects of national missile defense, it would be useful to take up the question of chemical and biological weapons since national missile defense has been touted as an important defense against them. Although chemical and biological weapons are fairly ineffective as weapons of mass destruction, many developing nations have them because they are effective as terror weapons. For example, Arab countries in the Middle East have explicitly talked of biological and chemical weapons as their atomic bomb when discussing Israel's nuclear deterrent. Neither biological weapons nor chemical weapons are by any means as lethal as nuclear weapons, which are the only effective military weapons of mass destruction.

Biological agents are notoriously sensitive to environmental factors such as drying and direct sunlight. They are best dispersed at night in a fine mist, upwind of the target, and within a restricted altitude range; if these conditions are not met, their effectiveness rapidly declines. Moreover, most lethal pathogens, with the exception of anthrax, have a limited lifetime so that their long-term storage in warheads is very difficult, if not impossible, to achieve. It has been reported, for example, that the Japanese cult Aum Shinrikyo (the Supreme Truth) tried at least nine times to use biological weapons by spraying lethal pathogens from trucks and rooftops. Not only did these attacks not cause a single fatality, they were hardly noticed. A July 2000 report of the British Royal Society, titled *Measures for Con-*

*trolling the Threat from Biological Weapons*, concluded that "the effectiveness of [biological weapons] spread in aerosol form against human populations in war or by terrorist activity has not been proven. . . . [I]t would seem prudent not to overestimate them."

Chemical weapons, unlike biological weapons, must be used in vast quantities to kill large masses of people. The Office of Technology Assessment reported to Congress in 1993 that a ton of sarin, perhaps the best-known chemical weapon, if dispersed over a heavily populated area against an unprotected population, could cause, under perfect weather conditions, between 3,000 and 8,000 deaths. If the sun were shining, or there was a wind, the number of deaths might be reduced to between 300 and 800. The perhaps incompetent release of sarin into the Japanese subway system by Aum Shinrikyo caused 5,000 casualties, but only 12 deaths. During the Iran-Iraq war, Iraq gassed some 27,000 Iranians, of whom 262 died. Chemical weapons are indeed terrible, but they are far from being "weapons of mass destruction." (WMD). As physicist Wolfgang Panofsky noted, after he pointed out the fragility of biological agents, "It is misleading to include chemical weapons in the category of WMD; 'weapons of indiscriminate destruction' or 'weapons of terror' might be a more appropriate designation."

Were such weapons to be used against the United States, it is not likely that intercontinental ballistic missiles would be involved. Terrorists are simply not likely to have access to such missiles as a delivery system, and it is unlikely that nations would waste ICBM capability on such ineffective weapons. If biological and chemical weapons *were* used by terrorists, or even by nations, less demanding means would be employed—drug shipments, suitcases, small boats—for which national missile defense would have no effect. The most effective means of delivery of biological and chemical weapons is a crop duster, and one should take careful note of the fact that small airplanes have defeated the warning systems and defenses of both the former Soviet Union and the United States: one landed in Red Square, and another deliberately crashed into the White House. Such means of delivery would be infinitely more accessible, cheaper, and in most cases, less traceable.

In the highly unlikely case that chemical and biological weapons were delivered by missile, the most effective method would be to divide the missile's payload into perhaps 100 bomblets or submunitions. Each would carry up to a few kilograms of chemical or biological agents. These agents can be protected from re-entry heating by the use of heat shield materials readily available to developing nations. The difficulties in defending against a missile using submunitions have already been noted; it is the same problem, of course, as in defending against a missile using decoys and chaff.

However, to enable the agents to be dispersed in a controlled manner upwind of the target, the attacker would still need to know the weather conditions at each target location, and have a missile whose trajectory could be altered in response to changing weather conditions. The missile would also have to have far greater accuracy than is within the present technical capacity of "nations of concern."

To summarize:

- Chemical and biological weapons are ineffective as weapons of mass destruction, and are unlikely to be used by nation states.
- Terrorists are highly unlikely to have access to intercontinental ballistic missiles.
- If chemical and biological weapons are used, other means of delivery are far preferable.
- If a ballistic missile were used as the delivery system, however, the use of submunitions would pose the same problems for defense as do decoys and chaff for nuclear weapons.

Rather than devote billions of dollars to national missile defense as a means of combating these weapons, the most effective effort the United States could devote itself to is to constrain the spread of these weapons through international agreements and workable verification procedures.

## THE TECHNOLOGY OF TESTING NMD

As we review the evidence, we can see that none of the national missile defense systems proposed over the past twenty years has ever proven in tests to be technically feasible, and that those presently under development are far from promising. It is highly unlikely that any candidate system can be shown to be militarily effective during the next eight years. That is, during the next two presidential terms neither the technology nor our testing methods will provide an assured capability to defeat long-range ballistic missiles. It is possible that President George W. Bush may decide to proceed with deployment of a national missile defense system during that time, but that decision will be based on political and economic considerations, which may include the perception that the threat justifies early deployment, not on demonstrated ability to defeat the likely threats.

Given the overwhelming advantage enjoyed by offensive nuclear forces, and the enormous technical difficulties inherent in any missile defense, this should not be surprising. It may be possible to someday construct a system that could provide at least some defense against intercontinental ballistic missiles. However, the United States is many years away from conducting the kinds of realistic tests that could provide military and political leaders with the minimum confidence they must have before risking the lives of millions of citizens.

The past two decades of efforts to invent a viable national missile defense have been characterized by exaggerated claims of success and promises of performance that later proved false. It is difficult to recall a missile defense proponent who *understated* the actual performance of a system. As we have seen, the problems began with the false claims of proponents of the X-ray laser that helped launch the SDI program in the early 1980s, including the claim that a single payload could stop an entire Soviet nuclear attack. Claims (see Chapter One) that the Patriot theater missile defense had proven itself in combat during the Gulf War were also false. Today false claims are made that cruisers, equipped with the Aegis radar system, and armed with existing missiles and kill vehicles, can quickly and inexpensively provide a highly effective defense against both intermediate- and intercontinental-range ballistic missiles.

Many experts and officials also maintain that countermeasures will not be significant obstacles to effective ballistic missile defense because we have already solved the discrimination problem. This is not true, despite some misleading claims of success (see above, and Appendices One and Two). For example, a test of the National Missile Defense interceptor, carried out on October 2, 1999, contained a test element where the interceptor was supposed to distinguish between the target and a decoy. Ballistic Missile Defense Organization officials provided important qualifying details of the test, in their pre-test briefings, that did not make it into their briefings after the test. The official news release by the assistant secretary of defense for public affairs on October 2 stated:

> The test successfully demonstrated "hit to kill technology" to intercept and destroy the ballistic missile target. An exoatmospheric kill vehicle

weighing about 120 pounds, equipped with two infrared sensors, a visible sensor, and a small propulsion system, located and tracked the target, guiding the kill vehicle to a body-to-body impact with the target and resulting in the target destruction using only the kinetic energy of the collision. This "hit to kill" intercept demonstrates that a warhead carrying a weapon of mass destruction—nuclear, chemical or biological—will be totally destroyed and neutralized.

Hitting a small target at these distances and speeds is a remarkable technological achievement, but not an unprecedented one, although the complexity of the system increases the chances that something will go wrong, a factor which cuts down on the system's reliability. Previous tests of similar interceptors have hit targets twice, in 1984 and in 1991. In both previous cases, as in this demonstration, the test plan and targets were optimized to ensure the likelihood of success. The October 2 news release neglected to mention four critical test enhancements:

• The target followed a preprogrammed flight path to a designated position.
• The interceptor missile also flew to a preprogrammed position.
• A Global Positioning Satellite receiver was placed on the target to send its position to ground control, and the necessary target location information was downloaded to a computer in the kill vehicle.
• The decoy released had a significantly different thermal signature than the target, making it easier for the sensors on the kill vehicle to distinguish between the objects.

Later analysis, disclosed by the *New York Times*, not by test officials, noted that the test had very nearly failed due to three other key problems:

• Incorrect star maps loaded into the kill vehicle's computer prevented the vehicle from ascertaining its position once it had separated from the booster.
• Back-up inertial guidance systems led to inaccuracies in pointing the sensors used to locate the target.
• The sensors finally saw the large, bright balloon decoy, re-oriented, continued searching, and located the cooler warhead that it had been programmed to recognize as the correct target.

For test purposes, there is nothing wrong with minimizing the number of variables in order to test key elements of the weapon system. The Global Position Satellite receiver, for example, was substituting for information that might be provided by future missile defense radars. It is vital, however, that test officials provide full disclosure of test limitations to policy makers at every stage of the process, lest test results be interpreted to have greater significance than, in fact, they do. The October 1999 test was much more a demonstration of two missiles intercepting each other than it was a test of intercepting an enemy missile under combat conditions. It proved only that a kill vehicle can intercept a target if it can see it.

Not only sophisticated issues are involved in the reliability of the system, but also basic engineering. For example, the interceptor failed to hit its target in the second intercept test, on January 18, 2000. Initial reports blamed the failure on faulty sensors. The latest analysis is that a leak in the gas lines used to cool the sensors may have caused the failure. This raises the obvious question: If a hand-built, meticulously prepared interceptor fails because of leaky tubing, how well are assembly-line production models likely to perform after sitting for years in the frozen Alaskan tundra? The third test in the series in July 2000 was also a failure, as the kill vehicle failed to execute a routine booster-separation maneuver. This again raised serious questions about the ability of the contractor to build reliable systems coordinating a large number of elements, all of which must perform perfectly, let alone a system that could actually discriminate between the real warhead and dozens of decoys.

Some officials, such as Department of Defense director of operational test and evaluation Philip Coyle, have tried to caution lawmakers on the tests. Director Coyle has warned that the test are "carefully scripted." In a recent annual report to Congress, he noted that the test program for a national missile defense system "is building a target suite that, while an adequate representation of one or two re-entry vehicles, may not be representative of threat-penetration aids, booster or post-boost vehicles."

Misinterpretation of test results is not an abstract concern. The last time the United States conducted a successful high-altitude, hit-to-kill intercept in the presence of decoys in 1991, the then-director of the Strategic Defense Initiative Office told Congress that the interceptor had determined on its own "which of the targets to go after, whether the decoy or the target." In his report to Congress, he claimed that the test "validates the concept of performing mid-course intercepts using basic discrimination techniques" and had discriminated between decoy balloons and the target warhead. These claims were false, as the General Accounting Office reported that Strategic Defense Initiative Office officials had consistently overstated the success of interceptor flight tests. The 1991 test also placed a device to guide the interceptor to the re-entry vehicle.

None of this information was disclosed to Congress until an investigation by the Government Operations Committee revealed the limitations of the test and the misrepresentations of success. Similarly, the single hit from four attempts during the Homing Overlay Experiment in the early 1980s was made possible only after the target was heated to 100 degrees Fahrenheit to increase its visibility to the interceptor's infrared sensors. Still, such tests go down in the books as successes, usually unqualified. The General Accounting Office report, cited above, found a pattern of misleading claims, forcing it to conclude that SDI officials had inaccurately portrayed four of five tests as successes, when they were not.

Equally relevant to the current debate, these inaccurate reports included claims that a space-based "Brilliant Pebbles" test was a "90-percent success," and was ready to proceed to more advanced testing. The General Accounting Office found that the "90-percent success" claim was based on a substantially downward revision of the original goals for the test, to correspond with what the interceptor was able to achieve, not what was originally planned. Of the original four goals, none was fully met, including the interceptor's ability to detect, acquire, and track a target. Since the program's "accomplishments were significantly less than planned," GAO concluded, the first phase of the program's testing "was completed only in the sense that Strategic Defense Initiative Office had decided to proceed into Phase II."

This history is part of the reason why it is common to hear advocates of missile defense claim that their proposed system is ready to go, inexpensive to build, and highly effective. In 1999, however, former Ballistics Missile Defense Organization director, Air Force General Lester Lyles, directly rebutted before the Senate the claims of the Heritage Foundation that effective sea-based missile defenses could be rapidly deployed. "When it comes to missile defense," he said, "there is nothing quick, cheap and easy." President Clinton rediscovered this truth when, despite large funding increases by both Congress and the administration over the previous four years, the technical problems with the proposed National Missile Defense system proved overwhelming.

## WASTE, FRAUD, AND ABUSE

Given that there is no signature that the exoatmospheric kill vehicle can use to distinguish between warheads and decoys, and that successful tests are needed politically for deployment, it follows that there is an enormous incentive for those who want to see the system deployed to rig the tests. And this is just what has been done.

As we mentioned briefly in Chapter One, a woman who had been a senior engineer at TRW, Dr. Nira Schwartz, charged the company with faking tests and evaluations of the kill vehicle's ability to discriminate warheads from decoys. These charges were backed up by other former TRW employees. Dr. Schwartz has filed a *qui tam* lawsuit under the False Claims Act, seeking to recover more than $500 million for the government, a part of which could be awarded to her. As she described the anti-missile system, "It's not a defense of the United States. . . . It's a conspiracy to allow them to milk the government."

The Pentagon's Defense Criminal Investigative Service looked into the claims, and Samuel W. Reed, the lead investigator, found it necessary to ask the Pentagon for an in-depth study of the issue. The outcome of Reed's investigations, which were "not based simply on allegations from Dr. Schwartz," is best summarized by quoting the *New York Times*: "Mr. Reed asserted that the Army had falsely reported to the Justice Department that he was against federal intervention. 'This statement has no factual basis,' he seethed." Mr. Reed formally closed his investigation of TRW on August 31, 1999, citing numerous "irregularities" and "discrepancies." He retired shortly thereafter.

While the TRW design has been relegated to the status of a backup in favor of one by Raytheon, recent tests show the Raytheon design to be not much better. This should be no surprise given the lack of a unique warhead signature distinguishing the warhead from a decoy. Even the Pentagon's former director of Operational Test and Evaluation, Philip Coyle, has faulted the anti-missile tests as insufficiently realistic "to support acquisition decisions."

Other evidence of possible fraud has been offered by MIT's Theodore Postol. In a letter to John Podesta, the Clinton White House chief of staff, dated May 11, 2000 (see Appendix Two), Postol informed the White House that the Ballistic Missile Defense Organization, in coordination with its contractors, attempted to hide the fact that the exoatmospheric kill vehicle would be defeated by the simplest of balloon decoys. They did this, Postol claimed, by tampering with both the data and analysis from the Integrated Flight Test-1A experiment. In addition, he charged that the Ballistic Missile Defense Organization modified the configuration of the follow-on flight tests to hide the program-stopping factors revealed in Integrated Flight Test-1A. After that test, data revealed that signals from some of the decoys were indistinguishable from the mock warhead, and those decoys were eliminated in planning for subsequent tests. In the end, there remained only a single large balloon decoy and a medium-sized warhead.

The evidence for these charges does not point merely to honest differences of opinion among scientists and engineers, but rather, according to Postol, to deliberate fraud. In particular, Postol has asserted that contractors, who work for and were paid and supervised by top-level Ballistic Missile Defense Organization management, deliberately removed data from the IFT-1A flight test that did not support their stated conclusion about the kill vehicle's ability to discriminate between decoys and warheads. Following the revelations that almost all of the decoys from the IFT-1A experiment could deceive the kill vehicle, Postol has charged that the Ballistic Missile Defense Organization altered the entire subsequent flight test program to conceal the fact that the kill vehicle could not deal with simple decoys. Further details of Dr. Postol's allegations are provided in Appendix Two, "Waste, Fraud, and Abuse," whose title comes from an executive order prohibiting the use of classification to hide waste, fraud, and abuse.

Postol alleges that the response to these accusations by Dr. Jacques Gansler, undersecretary for acquisition, technology, and logistics, raised serious questions about the competence of high-level Pentagon officials who were advising the president on missile defense, a problem that had also been chronic during the Reagan period. Gansler, after claiming to have forty years experience in the field of missile defense, said during a press conference that the National Missile Defense X-band radar was capable of measuring the mass of objects in the near vacuum of space, a claim that any high school physics student could refute.

In a letter to the president dated July 6, 2000, contained in Appendix Two, Postol stated that this and similar claims represent "more than just a random gap in knowledge; it goes to the heart of the matter, namely, pretending the system has the capability to distinguish between warheads and decoys in space, when in fact . . . it does not. . . . Dr. Gansler has stated his belief that improvements in 'software' will somehow make it possible to solve such discrimination problems in the future. But the simple truth [is that] no information can be extracted where there is none. If there is no reliable information in the signals created by warheads and decoys tumbling in space, if they have been disguised so as to emit signals that belie their physical characteristics, sophisticated software to interpret those signals will make no difference whatsoever." Such charges cut into the credibility of the anti-missile programs.

### THE SCHEDULING AND THOROUGHNESS OF TESTING NMD

Still another issue is the scheduling and thoroughness of the programs' testing. Noting that the NMD testing and development schedule is shorter than most other major system acquisition programs, the General Accounting Office warned in 1997 of the high risks inherent in the program:

> Because of the compressed development schedule, only a limited amount of flight test data will be available for the system deployment decision in fiscal year 2000. By that time, BMDO [Ballistic Missile Defense Organization] will have conducted only one system-level flight test, and that test may not include all system elements or involve stressing conditions such as targets that employ sophisticated countermeasure or multiple warheads. As a result, not all technical issues, such as discrimination, will be resolved by the time of the deployment review. Also the current schedule will permit only a single test of the integrated ground-based interceptor before production of the interceptor's booster element must begin. If subsequent tests reveal problems, costly redesign or modification of already produced hardware may be required.

By comparison, the only other U.S.-based ballistic missile defense system, the SAFEGUARD, had an acquisition schedule twice as long as planned for the NMD program. SAFEGUARD also had 111 flight tests, compared to only 3 intercept tests and 1 system-level flight test for NMD before a Fiscal Year 2000 deployment decision. The GAO noted that even this system-level test will not be comprehensive because it will not include all system elements, and that "the single integrated system test . . . will not assess the NMD system's capabilities against stressing threats such as those that use sophisticated countermeasures or multiple warheads. The test is to be conducted against a single target with only simple countermeasures such as decoys. No test against multiple warheads is planned."

Finally, there have been only fifteen intercept attempts outside the atmosphere conducted by the Department of Defense since 1982. Of these, only four, or 26 percent, actually hit their targets, and none demonstrated an ability to distinguish warheads from realistic decoys. The low number of past tests and the weak success rate warrant deep skepticism for much success with the proposed systems in the near future. Based on current schedules and all available evidence, it is reasonable to assume that if proposed high-altitude, ballistic missile defense systems are used in combat, they will fall far short of predicted effectiveness. In June 1998, the GAO reaffirmed its findings, concluding that, even with increased funding, technical and schedule risks are high.

## REASSESSING THE VIABILITY OF NATIONAL MISSILE DEFENSE

Some argue that, when President Clinton assumed office in 1993, he sabotaged plans that, if allowed to continue, by now would have produced a working and affordable missile defense. As we have noted, the Global Protection Against Limited Strikes (GPALS) plan, introduced by President George Bush and Defense Secretary Richard Cheney in January 1991, scaled back the original SDI program. It proposed, instead, a space-, sea-, and land-based system to destroy from 10 to 200 warheads "delivered by ballistic missiles launched from anywhere in the world to attack areas anywhere else in the world." The system relied heavily on the so-called "Brilliant Pebbles" space-based kinetic kill weapons, discussed earlier.

Some advocate a return to such a system today. But their confidence in the concept is based on faith, not fact. The Congressional Budget Office at the time estimated that the twelve-year cost of the GPALS plan would be at least $85 billion (in 1992 dollars). Annual expenditures would have averaged $8 billion. Since the system consisted largely of view graphs and concept studies, the Congressional

Budget Office pointed out that "the complexity of the Grand Forks and GPALS defenses suggests that total costs could exceed planned levels."

The General Accounting Office, in a report to the chairman of the Legislation and National Security Subcommittee in 1992, warned that the plan would have to "overcome tremendous technical challenges." This report was the last independent evaluation conducted of the GPALS program. It was not optimistic about the technical feasibility of the weapons proposed. "Such a system will push the cutting edge of technology," the General Accounting Office warned, adding that, "SDIO must rely on some technologies that are as yet unproven and learn how to integrate them into a reliable system." For the system to work, the GAO advised, "significant advances must be made over the next several years in critical areas," and that "if these advances are not achieved, schedule delays, escalating costs, and performance problems could occur." Even if the technologies became available, the analysts said, there was still "the enormous challenge of integrating them into a cohesive system." In short, space- and sea-based systems proposed in the waning days of the George Bush administration were hardly the ready-to-go defenses that advocates now fondly remember.

The track record of the tests of exoatmospheric hit-to-kill interceptors should indicate caution in projections of future capabilities. We have already noted the problems of possible misrepresentation or fraud. The other major problems, in addition to the basic issue of countermeasures, are the inadequacy and the poor results of the testing program. It is unlikely that the systems would completely fail in combat or in real situations, but the evidence indicates that they would perform significantly below either tested or predicted kill rates. Military commanders, therefore, would be wise not to base troop deployments or engagement strategies on unrealistic expectations of the protection these defenses will offer, or credit claims, such as those made for the Patriot theater missile system during the Gulf War, which fly in the face of facts (see Chapter One).

As the limitations of the National Missile Defense system proposed by President Clinton became clear, the conservative groups backing NMD began to tout other types of anti-missile defense. In the next chapter, we take up the basic problems associated with these systems, and why they are inadequate for national missile defense.

## NOTES

1. Phased-array radars are those which the Anti-Ballistic Missile Treaty allows only on the periphery of the signatory party's country. They can be directed electronically without physically moving the antenna.

2. For those who are mathematically inclined, the way these estimates are arrived at comes from the fact that each attempt to intercept an attacking missile is independent of any previous attempt, and the probability of intercept remains the same throughout each attempt. Under these conditions, if $q$ is the probability of failure, the probability of successfully intercepting the attacking missile at least once in $n$ tries is $1 - q^n$.

## RESOURCES

See "The Director, Operational Test and Evaluation, Department of Defense, FY 00 Annual Report," dated January 2001, prepared by Philip Coyle; and "Defense Acquisitions: Space-based Infrared Systems—Low at Risk," GAO-01-6, February 28, 2001.

George N. Lewis, Theodore A. Postol, and John Pike, "Why National Missile Defense Won't Work," *Scientific American* (August 1999), is a clear, readily understandable exposition of the technical problems surrounding National Missile Defense. George N. Lewis and Theodore A. Postol, "Future Challenges to Ballistic Missile Defense," *IEEE Spectrum* (September 1997), is a somewhat more technical presentation of the issues, with a concentration on exoatmospheric defenses. The article has excellent graphics and gives a clear presentation of the limitations of the army's Theater High-Altitude Area Defense (THAAD) and the navy's Theater-Wide System.

See Andrew M. Sessler (chair of the study group) et al., "Countermeasures: A Technical Evaluation of the Operational Effectiveness of the Planned US National Missile Defense System," a publication of the Union of Concerned Scientists, April 2000 (for access, see "Resources" for Chapter Four).

John Mueller and Karl Mueller, "Sanctions of Mass Destruction," *Foreign Affairs*, May/June 1999, is a pithy and penetrating commentary on the notion of weapons of mass destruction and the effect of sanctions.

Robert Oakley, "International Terrorism," *Foreign Affairs*, Winter 1986, is a very readable exposition on the different aspects of terrorism.

Wolfgang K. H. Panofsky, "Dismantling the Concept of 'Weapons of Mass Destruction,'" *Arms Control Today*, April 1998, adds a little realism to leaven one's reading.

A number of articles in the *New York Times* have exposed the testing problems of national missile defense. See, for example, "Flaws Found in

Missile Tests That U.S. Saw as a Success," January 14, 2000; "Missile Contractor Doctored Tests, Ex-Employee Charges," March 7, 2000; "Antimissile Testing Is Rigged to Hide a Flaw, Critics Say," June 9, 2000; and "Pentagon Gives a Preview of Missile Defense Test Tomorrow," July 6, 2000.

Some difficulties in interception are spelled out in "Strategic Defense Initiative: Some Claims Overstated for Early Flight Tests of Interceptors," (NSIAD-92–282).

For a shrewd assessment of biological weapons, see *Measures for Controlling the Threat from Biological Weapons*, British Royal Society, July 2000.

See also "Statement of LTG Lester Lyles, USAF, Director, Ballistic Missile Defense Organization, before the Subcommittees on Research and Development and Procurement, Committee on Armed Services, U.S. House of Representatives, February 25, 1999," and "Statement by LTG Ronald Kadish, USAF, Director, Ballistic Missile Defense Organization, before the Senate Armed Services Committee, June 29, 2000."

## Chapter Six

# Other Proposed National Missile Defense Systems

*Un sot trouve toujours un plus sot qui l'admire.*
[A fool always finds a bigger fool to admire.]

Boileu

In the waning days of the Clinton administration, numerous proposals surfaced for alternative forms of ballistic missile defense. Other than for the more exotic technologies that are far from proven, and which we will discuss later, these fall mainly into the categories of boost-phase defenses and late mid-course nuclear defenses. Some of the boost-phase proposals are based on an expansion of theater defenses, such as the army's Theater High-Altitude Area Defense (THAAD) and the navy's Theater-Wide System, both of which, like the National Missile Defense system proposed by President Clinton, are mid-course, exoatmospheric defenses.

These proposals have been advanced as alternatives to Clinton's NMD, which, the Republicans now claim, in the light of its failure to pass its most recent tests, was never a viable plan. Richard Perle, an advisor to President George W. Bush, summed up this assessment in a July 2000 op-ed piece in the *New York Times*: "The system's inadequacy is inherent in its technology and architecture. It relies on a small number of ground-launched interceptors, based on U.S. territory, that must be maneuvered with astounding precision to collide with incoming warheads at closing speeds of 15,000 miles per hour. Since each enemy missile may carry several nuclear warheads, along with a large number of decoys, the 100 interceptors could be overwhelmed. And the interceptors will have only one shot: there is no chance to fire a second time if an interceptor misses." He, too, noticed that the ground-based X-band radars, discussed in the last chapter, were highly vulnerable, and that "any nation capable of building long-range ballistic missiles and nuclear warheads could damage or destroy a large, immobile radar." Perle then went on to propose a sea-based, boost-phase defense.

## NUCLEAR DEFENSES

Before entering into a discussion of boost-phase defense, it is worthwhile to look at nuclear defense proposals that represent an important reason the Russians oppose national missile defense. They believe that, once the ineffectiveness of the system proposed by President Clinton is clear, the next logical step is to move to a nuclear-based system. The right wing in the United States has also made the point that nuclear-tipped interceptors are an acceptable option. For example, Frank Gaffney, director of the Center for Security Policy, in a press briefing organized by the Center for War, Peace, and the News Media on June 2, of 2000, claimed that "we can build a missile defense that will destroy not only incoming re-entry vehicles but decoys and all manner of other chaff and things intended to ensure that the warheads penetrate. The way you would do that is anathema to a great many people. . . . If we have to, we can absolutely, certifiably destroy incoming ballistic missiles by putting a small nuclear weapon on the front end."

Gaffney maintains that this "is the way that the Russians currently have their missile defense deployed around Moscow," although, as we have pointed out elsewhere in this book, during the Cold War, U.S. nuclear planners gave the Moscow defense system zero effectiveness in their targeting plans. There were essentially two reasons for this. The large phased-array radars located on the periphery of the Soviet Union, that the Galosh system relied upon for information needed to guide its battle management radars, would be destroyed early in a nuclear exchange. In addition, the defense would be simply overwhelmed by the number of warheads targeted into the area.[1]

The system being touted most strongly for nuclear-armed interceptors is one that would be mounted on ships. Even if such a system did offer greater assurance of destroying an incoming warhead, there are probably insurmountable political impediments to its deployment. Surface ships no longer carry nuclear weapons, and putting nuclear-armed interceptors on them would break an important barrier put into place by President George Bush, and possibly lead to the Russians re-deploying nuclear weapons on their ships.

The only navy platforms that still carry nuclear weapons are the ballistic missile submarines, and there are very good reasons, which we discuss later, why nuclear-armed or other types of interceptors should not be deployed on them. It would be difficult for the military to obtain timely release to launch nuclear-armed interceptors, and the resulting delay could impact their effectiveness. Nevertheless, the Russian defense planner must look not only at what is being proposed but also at what the system could become. If a hit-to-kill system will not work, the Russians may well be right that the temptation to move to a nuclear intercept will be irresistible to those committed to national missile defense.

Although there is some gain in using nuclear-tipped interceptors, they cannot give an acceptable probability of stopping an attacking warhead. The threat cloud, containing the incoming warhead, chaff, and decoys, would have had time to disperse over a considerable range, as the interception would not occur until late in mid-course. Accordingly, it would still be necessary to discriminate between chaff, decoys, and the warhead, a task which, as we have pointed out, is simply not possible. The reason for this is that even nuclear-tipped interceptors must be relatively close to knock out a warhead.

This can be understood from the nature of nuclear explosions in space. When a nuclear weapon explodes above the sensible atmosphere, the explosion emits almost entirely soft X-rays, along with some neutrons and gamma radiation. Soft X-rays cause damage because they produce superintense heat in the surface of any material they strike, which in turn generates a damaging shock wave that propagates into the material. The generated heat, however, diminishes with distance from the explosion. If they are not too close to the explosion, incoming nuclear weapons can be designed to survive not only the X-rays from a nuclear burst, but also the neutron emission that could damage the warhead by causing its plutonium or uranium to fission. Warheads that can survive a nuclear burst if they are not too close are said to be "hardened."

Deployment of an anti-missile system having nuclear-tipped interceptors to defend the United States would violate the Anti-Ballistic Missile Treaty, because the interceptors would have to be deployed in areas other than the nation's capitol and an ICBM field. Here the relevant provision is that "Each Party undertakes not to develop, test, or deploy ABM systems or components which are sea-based, air-based or mobile land-based." However, nuclear-tipped interceptors would also violate the Limited Test Ban Treaty of 1963. They would do so since no rational policy would deploy such a system without testing, and Article 1 of the Limited Test Ban Treaty prohibits the testing of nuclear weapons "in the atmosphere, beyond its limits, including outer space. . . ." The call for the deployment of nuclear interceptors by Frank Gaffney and others in the right wing of the Republican party can thus only be seen as an attack on the foundations of the arms control regime, which these two treaties represent.

From a political perspective, the proposal to use nuclear-tipped interceptors, and then test them, would also evoke the strong anti-nuclear sentiments which led to the Limited Test Ban and other anti-nuclear measures. Any administration trying to build domestic and international support for a national missile defense would pay a heavy price in pushing this option, which is probably why it has not been advanced by President Bush or members of his administration.

There are other reasons that mandate against the use of nuclear-armed interceptors. Nuclear explosions in space can damage satellites even though they are designed to withstand the radiation environment of space. When the United States carried out a series of nuclear tests in space during the early 1960s, there were no satellites. Today, much of the world depends on satellites for communication, weather, and surveillance.

## BOOST-PHASE DEFENSE

Boost-phase defense, that is, a defense that attempts to destroy missiles before they enter the upper atmosphere or outer space, is being advanced as an alternative to the Clinton model, and is far more acceptable to the Russians and the Chinese.

Why does Russia consider a boost-phase defense as nonthreatening? Why might China agree? The answer is simple: boost-phase defenses cannot readily be expanded to defend against more than a limited attack, and are probably ineffective against China's small arsenal because the interceptors cannot be located close enough to the Chinese launch points. Boost-phase defenses could, however, somewhat restrict Chinese ICBM deployment areas. How close to the launch point they must be located depends on a variety of factors, including the range and burn-time of Chinese ballistic missiles—factors that are also important for boost-phase defenses against North Korea, Iran, or other "states of concern."

If one believes some form of defense to be necessary, boost-phase defenses seem preferable. Whatever problems they may have in effectiveness, they do hold the advantage that it may be possible to deploy them without threatening the entire arms control regime. Because boost-phase defense does have some promise, as will be seen below, it is important to reiterate that the threat from the "states of concern" has been vastly exaggerated.

Boost-phase defense is also attractive because, unlike late mid-course or terminal defense, it is not necessary to use nuclear warheads, and because the booster provides a large signature that is easier to detect and target than systems designed to intercept missiles in mid-course, which can be disguised by decoys and chaff.[2]

The limited effectiveness of a boost-phase system, and, for that matter, the Clinton National Missile Defense system, does introduce an arms-race instability by giving a country wishing to maintain a credible missile strike force an enormous incentive to increase its number of missiles and look for ways to make them more effective. This is particularly true if the defense is not cost-effective at the margin. However, at least with respect to Russia, a sea-based boost-phase defense is less destabilizing than a land-based mid-course or terminal defense like NMD. This is due to the difficulty of rapidly expanding such a system because of the cost and lead time for building the many new ships it would require.

However, as we will see shortly, a realistic sea-based boost-phase interceptor is too large to fit on any of the standard navy combat ships. The only possibility is the Trident ballistic missile submarine—and from an operational point of view, such deployments may be a poor choice since they could compromise the invulnerability of the ballistic missile submarines by forcing them to operate in inappropriate, shallow coastal areas.

The ballistic missile submarines are the nation's ultimate assurance against nuclear attack, and a launch of any of their missiles, except from known test areas, has rarely occurred and would be taken by an adversary as a very serious event. Even if one were willing to compromise their vulnerability to some extent in this post–Cold War era, and allow ballistic missile submarines to carry interceptors and operate in inappropriate areas, there is the danger of confusing the launch of an interceptor with that of a ballistic missile. This would be true even if special submarines were designed for the interceptors, since there is no way to quickly tell what type of missile, intercontinental or interceptor, was launched. For example, during some tense period with China over Taiwan, what if China notified the United States and launched a missile carrying a communications satellite that veered off course, looking to our early warning systems like a single-missile attack? Would we believe it was a communications satellite? Not very likely. If we had a missile defense system, we would use it. The Chinese might interpret an interceptor launch to be a ballistic missile launch. Would they wait and see, or would they launch a retaliatory attack against the United States? Do we ever want to find out?

Because the boost phase is so short, boost-phase defenses make it virtually impossible for a human being, as opposed to a computer, to make the decision in time for an intercept. Boost-phase defenses are therefore critically dependent on what are known as the "rules of engagement," and the burn time of an enemy missile. It would be possible, since the interceptors are not nuclear armed, for the president and those high-level officials involved with making a launch decision (known as the National Command Authorities) to delegate the authority to launch, thereby eliminating the "man-in-the-loop." However, this should be given very careful consideration, particularly if the defense is sea-based and deployed on Trident submarines.

How much time is actually available? This obviously depends on a number of parameters, but if we use as a baseline a booster that has a burn time of about 250 to 320 seconds, comparable to the Titan II or Russian SS-18, the intercept will occur at about 200 seconds into the booster flight, if the interceptor is launched 120 seconds after the booster is launched. This assumes the distance between the two launch points is about 550 kilometers, and the interceptor has a 70-second burn time and an 8.5-kilometer-per-second burnout speed.[3] So there are about 120 seconds to detect the launch of the booster, make the decision to intercept, communicate that decision, and launch the interceptor.

How soon can we detect the launch of an ICBM? If one relies on satellite-based short wavelength infrared detectors (like the current Defense Support Program satellites in geosynchronous orbit), the booster must rise above about 10 kilometers before it can be seen. This happens at about 60 seconds after launch. So all the steps needed to launch the interceptor must take place in about 60 seconds. However, when a rocket motor first ignites, there is a large transient infrared signal, called the launch transient, which can be detected immediately, provided a wavelength is used that penetrates the atmosphere all the way to the ground. The difficulty is that one then can also see the background signal from the ground itself, but clever signal processing can subtract this background. So this "launch transient" can be used to detect the launch in less than a second, provided there is no thick, low-altitude cloud cover obscuring the launch area. The time available then is about 120 seconds, and if there is a thick cloud cover, only 60 seconds; not impossible, but very demanding.

However, it is also true that if we assume an adversary to have relatively primitive, liquid-fueled intercontinental ballistic missiles that take many hours to prepare for launch, it may be possible to observe these preparations. When this is the case (again, no heavy cloud cover), there could be additional warning time.

An adversary could significantly shorten the entire time if it could use solid-fueled boosters. These require very little preparation time to launch, and burn for a far shorter time than liquid-fueled boosters; that is, they have a much shorter boost phase. As an example, the United States can build fast-burn, solid-fueled boosters that carry multiple warheads and burn out at 80 to 90 kilometers after about 50 seconds. Such missiles were designed during the "Star Wars" era as a countermeasure to space-based "beam weapons." However, as noted in the last chapter, such solid-fueled boosters are probably well beyond the capability of "states of concern" for many years to come.

To summarize the example above, if there is no thick cloud cover in the launch area, and the launch transient is used to detect the launch, one has about 120 seconds available to detect the launch of the booster, make the decision to intercept, communicate that decision, and launch the interceptor. Without use of the launch transient, the time available is about 60 seconds.

Most proposals for boost-phase defense use a hit-to-kill technology like that of the proposed National Missile Defense system. What defeats the deployment of boost-phase defenses on combat ships is the increased weight of the kill vehicle due to its need to accelerate to track its target. Boost-phase defense is very different from mid-course defense, however, since one must intercept a booster that is *accelerating* so that its velocity is changing from second to second. Worse yet, the acceleration is not constant but varies over the course of boost phase.[4] What this means is that the kill vehicle deployed by the interceptor must be able to accelerate laterally—that is, in a direction at right angle to its path. The interceptor is guided to the *predicted* intercept point up to the time it releases the kill vehicle at burnout. This occurs some 70 seconds into the intercept trajectory. After the kill vehicle is released, one uses what is called "augmented proportional guidance" to track the accelerating booster until intercept. A more clever approach is to use a laser to illuminate the booster for about the last 30 seconds prior to impact, and home in on the reflected light. In either case, as we will see, the need to track a variably accelerating booster is a critical requirement, as it significantly increases the weight of the kill vehicle. This, in turn, determines the size of the interceptor needed to launch it and, therefore, the platforms upon which it can be deployed.

The general rule of thumb is that the kill vehicle should be able to laterally outaccelerate the rate at which it sees its target accelerating by a factor of two to three.[5] The bottom line is that, for most engagements, the kill vehicle must have a lateral acceleration of at least ten to fifteen times that of gravity; ten times gravity, or 10g, is minimal. Even so, the kill vehicle could easily miss the booster, although it could come close. For this reason, a fragmentation warhead (like that carried by the Patriot theater defense missile) may be necessary, thereby increasing the weight of the kill vehicle by some 150 to 170 pounds—and, as a result, the size of the interceptor.

What, then, is the weight of the kill vehicle, and what size interceptor is needed? The answer is not encouraging for proponents of ship-based boost-phased defenses. Because the kill vehicle needs more fuel and larger rocket motors than the vehicle designed for the Clinton NMD, the kill vehicle will weigh between 400 and 450 pounds, depending on whether a fragmentation warhead is needed. This compares to about 120 pounds for NMD. This means that the gross weight of the interceptor will be in the range of 30,000 to 40,000 pounds—compared, for example, to the navy Upper Tier interceptor's weight of 3,100 pounds. *This is a large missile, one that is not compatible with the storage and launch system on standard navy combat ships.* The only sea-based possibility is the Trident ballistic-missile submarine, and, as we have seen above, there are very good reasons one may not want to deploy ballistic missile defenses on these vessels.

In summary, the timeline for launching a boost-phase interceptor is very short, ranging from 60 seconds to 120 seconds at best. Because the kill vehicle must attack an accelerating booster, its weight is significantly larger than the one designed for the National Missile Defense system. This, in turn, means that the interceptor needed to launch it is so large that the interceptor cannot be deployed on navy combat ships, and if deployed at sea on existing ships, the only realistic choice is the Trident ballistic missile submarine. Doing so has significant negative policy impacts, and could raise serious survivability questions, depending on where the submarine is forced to operate.[6]

## THEATER DEFENSES

Let us turn now to the possibility of expanding theater defenses, such as the army's Theater High-Altitude Area Defense (THAAD) and the navy's Theater-Wide System. Both systems are designed for defense against intermediate-range ballistic missiles, and have been touted as forming the basis for a full national defense of the United States. A boost-phase defense that would expand existing theater missile defenses was also proposed by former CIA director John Deutch, former Secretary of Defense Harold Brown, and former Deputy Secretary of Defense John White in the Summer 2000 issue of *Foreign Policy*. They believe such an approach to be cheaper, technically mature enough for early deployment, and one for which it may be possible to negotiate changes in the ABM Treaty so that the defense could be politically acceptable to U.S. allies. These authors admit that "Chinese response to NMD deployment by the United States could prove even more damaging than any potential reaction from Russia." They dismiss Chinese concerns, however, by claiming that "a 10-fold increase in the Chinese ICBM force may be inevitable," clearly implying, without providing any justification, that the Chinese would increase their arsenal even if the United States did not deploy defenses, a position also taken by the Heritage Foundation. They further admit that U.S. theater missile defenses based on surface ships "to defend against North Korea could elicit Chinese concern about the proliferation of TMD [theater missile defense] in Northeast Asia (Taiwan, Japan, and South Korea)."[7]

Undismayed by these political problems, Deutch, Brown, and White go on to maintain that "no technical bright line separates NMD and TMD systems. A TMD system, for example, can intercept either a medium-range missile in terminal defense or even an ICBM, if positioned sufficiently close to the launch point to permit an intercept in the boost phase. Boost-phase intercept has the advantage of destroying missiles before separation of multiple warheads, decoys or submunitions that might contain biological or chemical agents." This claim that theater missile defenses are technically mature enough for early deployment as a boost-phase defense is seriously in error. The kill vehicles of both the army's THAAD and the navy's Theater-Wide System lack the necessary lateral acceleration capability needed for boost-phase intercept, as discussed above. Neither system can successfully attack a booster during its ascent. This is really the end of the story.[8]

Thus, while we concur with Deutch, Brown, and White that, "Based on military, technical, financial, and geopolitical considerations, we believe deployment of the present NMD system should be deferred," we find no promise in the deployment of a system based on expanding theater missile defenses. Existing theater defense systems are useless for boost-phase defense. Those who propose using them for this purpose have simply not done their homework. The Coyle Report, cited above, also makes clear that current theater systems are many years away from reliable deployment.

These considerations should give military commanders and policy makers low confidence in the ability of these systems to provide their troops, the nation, or U.S. allies any appreciable degree of protection against longer-range ballistic missile threats. Defense planners should consider whether more realistic schedules and elimination of duplicative programs could reduce the approximately $20 billion planned for missile defense efforts over the next five years, and whether the savings might be allocated to more pressing defense needs.

## EXOTIC APPROACHES

What, then, of the more exotic approaches to ballistic missile defense, such as the Air Force's Airborne Laser, mounted on a Boeing 747, or space-based lasers? Both approaches fail without even considering the technology because of their vulnerability. Anti-aircraft missiles *do* work, and the components of space-based defenses are sitting ducks for longer-range missiles. Space-based lasers also have to be in the right place when a missile is launched. Since they have to be in low earth orbit to maximize the energy they can put on the missile, to always have one in the right place to destroy an attacking missile means there must be a very large constellation of lasers in space. Not only are a large number of expensive laser battle stations needed, but a space-based laser defense is impractical in any case since the lasers are themselves large and vulnerable. The need for a large constellation is the same problem faced by Lawrence Livermore National Laboratory's "Brilliant Pebbles" fantasy. Space-based "Brilliant Pebbles" have a very limited engagement range leading to the need for far more of them in orbit. This game gets very expensive, very quickly. Still another problem is that space-based systems would violate the 1967 Peaceful Uses of Outer Space Treaty and set a dangerous precedent of weaponizing outer space.

For those interested in the technical perspective, high-power lasers cannot operate very effectively in the atmosphere. There are fundamental limitations having to do with the propagation of light through the air's gases. First of all, the atmosphere is turbulent. This turbulence can cause the laser beam to spread, limiting the amount of energy that can be deposited on a target. Much of the work on military lasers has tried to get around this awkward fact. One approach is to use what are known as "adaptive optical techniques," which compensate for atmospheric turbulence. This is the same technique used by some of the large astronomical telescopes. Adaptive optics uses light reflected from the target to determine the atmospheric defocusing of the reflected beam due to the turbulence. It then mechanically bends the mirror used to project the high-intensity beam to compensate for the determined defocusing. This approach has its limitations. Primary among them is "spoofing," where the missile uses countermeasures to confuse the adaptive optical system.

Another problem arises for adaptive optics when the target missile has a large enough velocity perpendicular to the laser beam. When this happens, the high-intensity beam will travel over a different path than that traveled by the reflected light from the missile, which was used by the adaptive optics to adjust the mirror. To put it another way, the light received from the missile, which is used to cue the adaptive optics, and the powerful laser beam intended to destroy the missile will travel in the air along separate paths that have different turbulence characteristics. The end result is that the adaptive optics won't work.

In addition to turbulence, propagation of high-intensity laser beams through the atmosphere is limited by a phenomenon given the colorful name of "thermal blooming." This is where absorption by the atmosphere of some of the energy in the high-intensity beam heats the air within the beam's confines, thereby changing what is called its index of refraction, so that the beam diverges. This is very much like the distortion one can see when looking at an object across a hot plate or toaster—the image of the object shimmers. There is even an effect that, at high intensity, can work the other way and help propagate the beam in the atmosphere (at least above three kilometers in altitude). This is the phenomenon of "bleaching," where the ability of the molecules comprising the air to absorb energy decreases.

When all is said and done, lasers must dwell on their targets for as long as it takes to deposit the energy needed to destroy them. The longer this is, the more difficult it is to keep the laser beam on the target. To minimize the effects of thermal blooming, high-energy lasers often attack their targets with repetitive pulses. However, this means that they must track the target for a longer period, in order to deposit sufficient energy to destroy it. Such tradeoffs, which limit system performance, are common.

Boost-phase laser weapons are also subject to straightforward countermeasures. Simply spinning the booster is one trick. If one is willing to accept a small penalty in payload, a layer of "ablative" heat shield material can be applied to the booster skin. Such material shields the booster by carrying away heat by burning, rather than allowing the heat from the laser beam to penetrate to the missile skin. Ablative coatings can even be applied to existing boosters. Depending on the laser's wavelength, it may be possible to increase the reflectivity of the missile skin so that much of the incident energy is simply reflected.

To summarize, the problems that beset boost-phase laser defenses are their vulnerability, the difficulty of propagating sufficient energy through the atmosphere, and the fact that there are simple countermeasures to laser attack. Exotic defenses are still very much at the research stage, and have remained there for well over twenty years!

## NOTES

1. The Russian defenses around Moscow, like all terminal defense systems, are crucially dependent on radar targeting information. During the Soviet era, a broad network of radars, known picturesquely as "Hen House" radars, were deployed around the periphery of the Soviet Union. These were meant to provide early warning and warhead acquisition information to the "Dog House" radars located in the Moscow region. The Hen House radars were vulnerable not only to nuclear attack, but would be "blinded" by nuclear detonations since they operated in the very high frequency (VHF) part of the radio frequency spectrum.

The Dog House radars, later supplemented by Cat House radars, provided battle management for the Moscow defenses, assigning targets and target acquisition information to the tracking radars and interceptors. While both the Dog House and Cat House facilities are large phased-array radars capable of handling a number of targets simultaneously, their effectiveness against a full-scale U.S. attack was essentially nil. Not only would the number of attacking weapons rapidly saturate the system, but target acquisition could easily be denied by the use of exoatmospheric chaff, which would conceal the location of the re-entry vehicles from the target acquisition radars. Such countermeasures remain effective even in the case of an attack by a small number of warheads.

2. A number of Department of Defense analyses show that staring sensors (those that produce a single image of the missile and its plume or flame), operating at medium-wave infrared wavelengths, are capable of observing both the plume and body of a missile in powered flight. However, the *New York Times* reported in June 2000 that Secretary of Defense Cohen "asserted that it would be hard to develop . . . interceptors that could distinguish between a missile's flame and the missile itself and hit it in time." The fact that this assertion is not true suggests that Secretary Cohen was trying to protect the existing approach to missile defense.

3. The numerical data for much of this chapter are taken from an analysis by Theodore Postol of the MIT Security Studies Program.

4. For the example we are using, the baseline booster burns for 250 seconds and has two stages, the first of which burns out at 115 seconds, that is, after the interceptor deploys the kill vehicle. The kill vehicle, deployed at 70 seconds after launch of the interceptor, sees the acceleration of the booster vary from about 2.6 gravities to 6.5 gravities at first-stage burnout. The acceleration of the booster, now driven by the second stage, varies from 1.5 gravities to 7.6 gravities at second-stage burnout at 250 seconds. (Accelerations are measured in terms of the acceleration of dropped objects near the earth's surface, which by definition is 1 gravity.)

5. The acceleration observed by the kill vehicle depends on the angle

made between the trajectory of the booster and the trajectory of the interceptor. This is greatest when the interceptor's trajectory is at a right angle to the trajectory of the booster, which is rarely the case.

6. In addition to problems with sea-based NMD discussed above, the Center for Defense Information cites several others: "1) The ship must be properly positioned so that its intercept envelope overlaps the threat missile's flight envelope. Ships positioned off North Korea's coast, for instance, would have difficulty trying to knock down an ICBM launched from that country over the North Pole. 2) To be properly positioned for intercept, ships would be confined to a relatively small 'box,' making the vessel easier to locate and attack. 3) The ship's crew would have to be at continuous 'battle stations' to ensure that a defensive strike during boost phase could be executed at any time. The option of frequently rotating ships would require a number of additional ships—probably three for every one on station—which would rapidly add to NMD costs." See "National Missile Defense: *What Does It All Mean?* A CDI Issue Brief," September 2000.

7. U.S. theater defenses, not theater defenses employed by U.S. allies, are what are under discussion. The thing to keep in mind when considering theater defense in Northeast Asia is that real defense of these countries, as they well know, depends on maintaining U.S. involvement. Their national interest lies in being strongly coupled to the United States, not in having their relationships weakened by having their own theater missile defenses. However, in April 2000, President Clinton made clear the United States would not provide an advanced theater missile defense system to Taiwan, and in May, Taiwan's new defense minister, Wu Shihwen, announced that Taiwan would develop a missile defense system unilaterally, banking on sufficient funding and technological progress.

8. There is another reason these systems are not good for boost-phase defense. Both systems were designed to intercept warheads in *late mid-course*, in the near vacuum of space. As a result, their infrared sensors are of the wrong type to optimally track a missile in boost phase, when it is still burning its fuel. Both use detectors intended to operate in the long-wave infrared region of the spectrum, so that they can detect the essentially room-temperature heat emissions from a warhead in space. Boost-phase would require detectors designed to be used in the short to medium wave part of the infrared spectrum.

## RESOURCES

Many of the more exotic anti-missile defense schemes were examined in detail during the "Star Wars" years. Those reports that were particularly useful are given below in the order of their appearance. All of them are at a level accessible to the general reader.

The first independent analysis was done by Ashton B. Carter, who was then at the Massachusetts Institute of Technology, for the U.S. Office of Technology Assessment. It was a background paper, titled "Directed Energy Missile Defense in Space," published in April 1984. It includes an appendix on the ABM Treaty and related documents.

The second chapter of the March 1984 report by the Union of Concerned Scientists, "Physics and Geometry versus Secrecy and Clairvoyance," is a delight to read. A very good introduction relegates technical material to appendices. The report is available from the U.S. Office of Technology Assessment.

Two reports by the Office of Technology Assessment, "Ballistic Missile Defense Technologies" and "Anti-Satellite Weapons, Countermeasures, and Arms Control," were published in a single volume by Princeton University Press in 1986 under the title *Strategic Defenses*. It is a comprehensive study that discusses many relevant strategic issues. The reader will find the glossary of acronyms and terms very useful.

The Strategic Defense Initiative Organization published a report to Congress on March 13, 1989, "Strategic Defense Initiative," that covers the program in great detail. The reader should note the almost total elimination of the nuclear driven X-ray laser from the program. The SDIO volume is well worth reading, since now—over ten years later—the reader may judge its credibility and perhaps calibrate current Ballistic Missile Defense Organization claims.

For a hostile assessment of the missile defense system supported by the Clinton administration, see Richard Perle, "A Better Way to Build a Missile Defense," *New York Times*, July 13, 2000. For former Secretary of Defense William S. Cohen's views on missile defense, see the *New York Times*, June 14, 2000. See also John Deutch, Harold Brown, and John P. White, "National Missile Defense: Is There Another Way?" *Foreign Policy*, Summer, 2000. For Frank Gaffney's enthusiasm for nuclear anti-missiles, see "Global Beat Issue Brief," No. 59, June 2, 2000, at *http://www.nyu.edu/globalbeat/pubs/ib59.html*.

# PART III

## INTERNATIONAL CONSEQUENCES AND POLICY ALTERNATIVES

## Chapter Seven

# Geopolitical Implications of National Missile Defense

The debate on national missile defense has revolved around the feasibility and dependability of a deployable system, but far more serious problems should concern decision makers in Washington. Should such a system work or, more likely, should the international community perceive that the United States can make it work, a series of national security problems will ensue. Ties between Russia and China will improve; the angry reaction of our European allies will weaken our leadership of the NATO alliance; America will weaken its own counterproliferation and arms reduction policies and the salutary effects of these policies; and the United States will lose its limited leverage on the strategic policies of India and Pakistan. Thus, any U.S. decision to pursue national missile defense will have negative consequences for all aspects of U.S. national security and strategic deterrence.

The Anti-Ballistic Missile Treaty, completed in 1972, was based on the proposition that, in the long run, offensive strategic forces could counter any innovations that strategic defense might offer. As reported in Lawrence Freedman's *The Evolution of National Strategy*, both sides accepted the view of former Secretary of Defense Robert McNamara, that "No meaningful victory is even conceivable in a third unlimited world war, for no nation can possibly win a full-scale thermonuclear exchange. The two world powers that have now achieved a mutual assured-destruction capability fully realize that." The ABM Treaty specifically banned a space-based defense, and ruled out not just deployment but developmental testing for a national missile defense. The text of the treaty dealt primarily with verification; laboratory research was permitted because such research could not be monitored. Each side agreed to rely on its surveillance and detection systems to monitor the other's compliance not just with the treaty but with an interim five-year agreement that set the ceiling on long-range missile launchers. Also, the agreement forbade either side to interfere with the other's surveillance systems or conceal those activities that had to be monitored.

Arms control advocates and international lawyers have considered the ABM Treaty the backbone of the arms control regime and an obvious barrier to President Reagan's Strategic Defense Initiative or any current deployment of a national missile defense. The international community obviously shares that view. Unlike the SALT I Treaty, which was controversial because it did not halt the arms race, there were no significant quarrels with the ABM Treaty, which was ratified in the Senate with only two dissenting votes. As John Newhouse makes clear in his *War and Peace in the Nuclear Age*, senior disarmament negotiators Paul Nitze and Paul Warnke, who disagreed on most aspects of arms control, agreed on the importance of the ABM Treaty and were proud of the fact that they "delivered" the Pentagon on the treaty.

Since the ratification of the treaty, there has been agreement among a wide range of senior American foreign policy experts that it is the keystone of American disarmament and deterrence policy, and should remain sacrosanct. Retired Senator Sam Nunn fought off presidential efforts to reinterpret or rescind the treaty. In 1985, in response to President Reagan's stated desire to build an anti-missile defense system, former secretaries of defense Robert S. McNamara, Clark M. Clifford, Elliot L. Richardson, Melvin R. Laird, James R. Schlesinger, and Harold Brown warned Moscow and Washington to "avoid actions that would undermine the ABM Treaty."

Several days after the former secretaries issued their strong statement in support of the treaty, President Reagan's former national security advisor Robert McFarlane advanced a new and "broad" interpretation of a key provision of the ABM Treaty that would permit development and testing, though not deployment, of space-based

ABM systems and components that were banned by the treaty. According to Ambassador Raymond L. Garthoff, who has written widely and authoritatively on these issues in *The Great Transition*, McFarlane had never discussed the reinterpretation with President Reagan, and it had not been considered by the government's national security agencies or by those who negotiated the treaty. A unilateral reinterpretation of the treaty would undermine American credibility abroad and would violate the balance of powers established in the U.S. Constitution, if the executive branch unilaterally reinterpreted a treaty that had been ratified by the Senate.

McFarlane's remarks brought a hailstorm of criticism both from within the Reagan administration and from the Western alliance, and eventually forced the Reagan administration to backtrack. Secretary of State George Shultz objected strongly, and hinted at a threat to resign over the issue. The European states uniformly opposed any reinterpretation, and West German Chancellor Helmut Kohl and British Prime Minister Margaret Thatcher sent critical letters to President Reagan. As a result of the criticism, Reagan authorized Secretary Schultz to state that the administration would continue to limit testing and development of its Strategic Defense Initiative according to the traditional "restrictive" interpretation of the treaty. The restrictive view would ban even the most minimal steps to construct parts of a missile defense, including laying concrete or raising walls for a system. But there was no commitment on how long the administration would continue to abide by the restrictive interpretation.

The Clinton administration flip-flopped on the issue. It initially abandoned the Reagan administration's "reinterpretation" of the ABM Treaty; as late as October 1999, President Clinton said that "I do not want to throw out the ABM Treaty." But, in a surprising twist, White House, Pentagon, and State Department lawyers announced in June 2000 that the United States could begin building the first piece of the National Missile Defense system without violating the treaty. The lawyers argued that workers could not only clear trees and dig dirt at the proposed radar site on Shemya Island in the western Aleutians, but that contractors could pour a concrete pad without violating the treaty. When asked how the administration could suddenly change the threshold for violating the treaty, a senior Pentagon official attributed it to "better lawyers." President Clinton was briefed on the new interpretation before his summit meeting with President

Vladimir Putin in early June, but reportedly chose not to raise the issue on that occasion. The Russians would certainly consider even groundbreaking for a defense system a violation of the ABM Treaty. The argument of the new Bush administration that the treaty is null and void because it was signed with the Soviet Union is specious, as Russia is clearly the legal inheritor of obligations undertaken by its predecessor.

The Bush administration, meanwhile, has decided to ignore the international opposition to a national missile defense and move pell-mell toward a strategic defense initiative that will involve the abrogation of the Anti-Ballistic Missile Treaty. Leading officials from Europe, Asia, and Latin America have expressed significant opposition to the idea of strategic missile defense, but this did not stop Secretary of Defense Donald Rumsfeld from traveling to Western Europe less than three weeks after the inauguration of the new president to proclaim the new administration's determination to deploy national missile defense. Rumsfeld told the European members of NATO that the Bush administration was determined to deploy a national missile defense, and the European representatives replied without exception that the United States was moving too fast and that these moves would touch off a new and dangerous arms race. London's centrist newspaper *Independent* said it best on February 2, 2001, noting that the case against NMD was "simple: It is expensive, it is unproven, it will destabilize arms control efforts, and it does not even meet the most likely threat scenarios from rogue nuclear states." The Western and Japanese press were particularly concerned with "triggering a new arms race," and even the South Koreans are worried that U.S. plans will lead to North Korea's revival of its long- and medium-range missile programs.

## NEGATIVE RESPONSE FROM RUSSIA AND CHINA

Moscow and Beijing consider a national missile defense system an attempt to gain "unilateral military and security advantages" as well as a violation of the ABM Treaty. They warn that breaching the ABM Treaty would "trigger a new arms race." Russian President Vladimir Putin emphatically stated that any move to withdraw from the treaty will lead Russia to treat all existing U.S.-Russian arms agreements as null and void. China's chief arms negotiator, Sha Zukang, of the Chinese Foreign Ministry's department of arms control and disarmament, warned that if Washington went ahead with an NMD deploy-ment designed to intercept "tens of warheads"—a figure suspiciously close to the eighteen to twenty single-warhead ballistic missiles that represent China's entire nuclear deterrent capability—Beijing would not sit on its hands.

Sino-Russian joint opposition to either a U.S. effort to deploy a national missile defense system or a reinterpretation of the ABM Treaty has led to improved bilateral relations between the two na-tions. During a summit meeting in July 2000, President Putin and President Jiang Zemin issued a joint statement denouncing U.S. plans on missile defense, and vowed to strengthen their strategic partner-ship.

U.S. policies have, in fact, been one of the primary forces driving China and Russia together. The U.S. decision to expand NATO, seen as aimed at Moscow, led to a renewal of Russian interest in forming a strategic relationship with its eastern neighbor. China, which has similar concerns regarding a U.S. policy to contain Beijing and pro-tect Taiwan, has fostered closer ties with Russia.

Both see definite advantages in improving bilateral relations and creating at least the impression of a strategic partnership. Moscow hopes the impression of rapprochement will convince the United States that the Kremlin is not without geopolitical options. On a regional level, Moscow wants to improve relations with China in or-der to get better control of the Chinese emigration problem on the Sino-Russian border. Since the dissolution of the Soviet Union, Mos-cow has been concerned with increased Chinese immigration into the impoverished Russian Far East region, where hundreds of thousands of Russians live close to a region with hundreds of millions of Chi-nese. Russia, faced with the prospect of further expansion from NATO on its western frontier, must improve relations in the east.

Beijing has its own reasons for improving relations with Russia. The Chinese share the world's longest frontier with Russia, and Bei-jing must improve its security relations in the north in order to con-centrate on its future security concerns with Taiwan. Faced with the possibility of U.S. containment of China, reinforced by a proposed U.S. national missile defense, Beijing must maintain a stable and pre-dictable strategic relationship with Russia.

At the same time, historic suspicions limit the extent of the part-nership between Russia and China. The Chinese have never had any genuine respect for the Russians (and the Putin government knows this); at the same time, Beijing must be concerned that even the perception of improved Sino-Russian ties would encourage Japan to improve its strategic relationship with the United States. Beijing, of course, wants to avoid a closer U.S.-Japan relationship.

Russian opposition to NMD is based on Moscow's traditional concerns that the United States might create a first-strike capability for its strategic forces. As far as Moscow is concerned, the ABM Treaty meant that the United States and the Soviet Union had surrendered any meaningful right to defend their own territory and societies against the other's nuclear weapons. In January 1999, a top Russian general accused the United States of exaggerating the threat from so-called "rogue states" and of violating its treaty commitments. The Russian foreign ministry issued a statement calling the deployment plan a "serious threat to the whole process of nuclear arms control as well as strategic stability."

Once again, as in the Reagan period (see Chapter One), the Kremlin is faced with the uncertainty of a U.S. national missile defense and, once again, Russia's leaders may be forced to rely on their own offensive systems to counter the challenge. While the Russians have stated that they would like to reduce the nuclear arsenals of the Russian Federation and the United States eventually to a level of 1,000 strategic warheads, it is unlikely that they would do so if the United States goes ahead with NMD. Thus, both countries would be locked into unnecessarily large nuclear weapons inventories for the foreseeable future unless unilateral reciprocal reductions take the place of agreements.

The Russians also could increase their offensive capability. They could return multiple warheads to their strategic missiles, thus rejecting a major provision of START II, and could deploy additional countermeasures on their missiles that could penetrate the NMD system. The new Topol missile system was initially designed to carry MIRVs (multiple independent re-entry vehicles), thus magnifying their threat. Moscow could also resort to shorter-range tactical nuclear weapons, which could be used to threaten key European states or forward-deployed U.S. forces, thus putting at risk the disarmament successes since the Intermediate-Range Nuclear Forces Treaty in 1987.

A more antagonistic relationship between Washington and Moscow also could put at risk the excellent verification and monitoring systems that the two nations have forged, including intrusive on-site inspection. Russian-American arms control and verification architecture would be threatened by any national missile defense system, even one that was technologically flawed. Rarely has so much international cooperation been placed at risk for the promise of so little.

Finally, if the United States were to reinterpret or abrogate the ABM Treaty, and Russia was prepared for a serious worsening of relations with the United States, Moscow could withdraw from the Intermediate-Range Nuclear Forces Treaty. The commander-in-chief of the Russian Strategic Missile Forces, Marshal Vladimir Yakovlev, told the graduating class of the Peter the Great Missile Academy in the year 2000 that "all the requisite scientific, economic, military, and technical feasibility studies have been prepared" for such a withdrawal. Moscow would proceed cautiously in this direction, however, because the United States has far greater financial and industrial potential for restoring its intermediate- and short-range missiles in Europe than exists in Russia today.[1]

At the very least, NMD has given the Russians a diplomatic opportunity that President Putin has been quick to exploit. In a very short period of time in the summer of 2000, he traveled to Germany, China, and North Korea to try to build a multipolar world against American influence, forge common positions against NMD, and create bilateral platforms against its deployment. In Germany, Putin introduced the notion of a joint defense system with Europe, which forced Germany and other European states to respond directly to European missile defense issues. On a whirlwind tour of Asia, he arranged for a strong joint statement with China against NMD, and stole a march on the United States by gaining a Pyongyang statement that it might drop its strategic weapons programs.

At the same time, Putin is working effectively to moderate Russia's policies, particularly after the disastrous results of the second war in Chechnya. He has no illusions about reversing Russia's imperial decline, and has been coaxing Russian generals who command both nuclear and conventional forces that they will have to do with fewer of both. Finally, he wants to tackle international problems collectively at the United Nations and not in direct opposition to the United States and its Western allies. Opposition to national missile defense also has presented Putin with an international platform for criticizing and isolating the United States.

Chinese opposition to U.S. national missile defense and theater missile defense is genuine and fundamental. Russia, with its thousands of strategic warheads, could not be stymied by a limited national missile defense that initially promises to be effective against only two dozen incoming missiles. But China, with no more than twenty intercontinental strategic missiles, must be concerned with even a limited defense network in the United States. As a result of U.S. pursuit of a national missile defense, China has begun to debate the wisdom of its policy of no-first-use of nuclear weapons, and may reverse its previous decision not to develop multiple warhead missiles. The aim of its last nuclear test series was reportedly to develop missiles that could carry multiple warheads, but which would not be independently targetable.

Chinese opposition to national and theater missile defense is also a reflection of Beijing's obsessive concern with a U.S. strategy of containment of China, and with China's need to be the regional security manager in Northeast Asia. China does not want to envisage the United States coming to the defense of Taiwan or deploying a tactical missile defense in Taiwan against China's military forces. A U.S.-sponsored missile defense in either Japan or Taiwan would mean a loss of leverage for Beijing in Northeast Asia. Any U.S. challenge to China's strategic position in the Asian theater—particularly regarding Taiwan—would allow the United States to challenge Beijing's strategic role in the region and thwart its interest in ultimately integrating Taiwan.

China views national missile defense as a demonstration of U.S. efforts to secure its global military position and to achieve "absolute security," according to Professor Paul Godwin of the National War College. China's fundamental concerns over the Taiwan issue have produced equally strong opposition against a theater or tactical missile defense on behalf of Taiwan. U.S. aircraft carriers and a theater missile defense (TMD) would complicate Chinese military planning, particularly in view of the relative lack of sophistication of much of its weaponry. Beijing's leaders would have to assume that the deployment of a TMD would give the United States more reason to protect Taiwan's sovereignty, or risk escalation in case of a Chinese attack. The Chinese already are positioning medium-range missiles on the coast of the Fujian province opposite Taiwan in response to any U.S. commitment to proceed with a missile defense there. As a result of recent Chinese force deployments, the United States may have already worsened the strategic position of its ally, Taiwan, merely by discussing a possible decision to deploy a missile defense. Presumably China will be able to overwhelm any theater missile defense in Taiwan with barrage attacks and the use of countermeasures.

China would perceive any U.S. deployment of TMD in Taiwan as a resumption of the U.S. military alliance with Taipei, abrogated in 1978 as a condition of the historic rapprochement between Washington and Beijing. China regards Taiwan as a renegade province and believes that U.S. strategic weaponry in Taiwan would encourage Taipei to formally declare its independence. As a result, U.S. scholars on China, as well as former senior Department of Defense officials such as John Deutch, Harold Brown, and William Perry, share the view that national missile defense would have a decisively negative impact on U.S.-Chinese relations. At the very least, Beijing would increase its defense spending and curtail cooperation on arms control and nonproliferation.

China also fears a closer strategic relationship between the United States and Japan. The United States and Japan are working together on a TMD program for Northeast Asia, and it is unlikely that Japan would develop a localized theater missile defense without U.S. help and technology, as well as a U.S. commitment to go ahead with its own system. Some Chinese officials have suggested that Beijing would accept a low-tier (terminal or late mid-course) missile defense in Japan as a system to protect U.S. bases from any North Korean weapons programs. But China opposes a high-tier system as the basis for the remilitarization of Japan, an end to U.S. constraint on Japanese policy, and a possible link to protecting Taiwan from Chinese attacks. In any event, some Chinese officials link U.S. plans for a national and theater missile defense, and consider Japanese assistance in developing a theater missile defense as a technological boost to U.S. efforts to deploy national missile defense.

In addition to deploying offensive weapons against Taiwan, China is threatening to undermine the architecture of its arms control policy and walk away from nonproliferation agreements with the West. Beijing's top arms control negotiator, Sha Zukang, has warned that the sale of U.S. technology to Taiwan for a TMD system would "lead to serious confrontation" and a renunciation of previous undertakings barring nuclear or chemical weapons proliferation and nuclear testing.

In fact, China already has taken practical steps to block U.S.-backed disarmament proposals because of the missile defense issue. In Geneva, the Chinese have been holding up talks at the Conference on Disarmament on a treaty to stop production of fissile material. Instead, the Chinese negotiators want to focus on a treaty to limit or control space-based weapons systems, which could be part of an expanded U.S. multitiered missile defense scheme. Sha Zukang stated specifically that Beijing would link its attitude toward nonproliferation and modernization of its nuclear forces to developments in the U.S. National Missile Defense program.

In addition to compromising the expanding arms control dialogue between the United States and China, a national missile defense would lead to increased deployments of Chinese strategic weapons. Beijing is well placed to increase its numbers of strategic warheads, as well as to deploy multiple-warhead missiles to overwhelm any NMD. The 2000 NIE suggests that the size of China's ICBM force could grow from the current level of 18 to 20 to as many as 200 ICBMs, including the DF-41, which is a road- and rail-mobile solid-fuel system. U.S. experts on China believe that some incremental modernization of China's missile forces is likely in any event, but that the timing and scope of these efforts will be determined by U.S. decisions on national missile defense. A theater missile defense would almost certainly lead to Chinese deployment of additional medium-range missiles targeted against Taiwan.

At the very least, a national or theater missile defense system would bring an end to Washington's limited leverage in controlling or limiting China's technological assistance to the missile programs of Iran and Pakistan. China has provided Pakistan with the design for a nuclear weapon, and has sold missiles or missile technology to Pakistan, Iran, Libya, and Saudi Arabia. In 1998, Pakistan detonated a nuclear device, and, in July 2000, Iran tested a medium-range ballistic missile, creating additional concerns about China's sharing of missile technology. The deployment of NMD could lead to reversal of the Chinese decision in 1994 to stop selling M-11 missiles to Pakistan and to abide by the guidelines of the Missile Technology Control Regime, which China has not formally joined. In any event, a U.S. national missile defense will lead China to share more—and not less—nuclear and missile technology with other states.

## OPPOSITION IN SOUTH ASIA

If China were to increase its arsenal and walk away from nonproliferation, it is very likely that Pakistan and India, both of which detonated nuclear devices in May 1998, would do the same. New Delhi has warned that any increases in the Chinese strategic arsenal would lead directly to enhancements of India's triad of land-, air-, and sea-based nuclear assets. Pakistan, of course, states that it will match India's moves, and some sources already believe that Islamabad's nuclear arsenal is far larger than previously suspected—perhaps larger than the arsenal in India. Pakistan, moreover, has never considered a no-first-use pledge regarding nuclear weapons, and its senior officials have declared recently that "There is no way Pakistan can hold out any assurance that it will not use any nuclear weapons if its existence is threatened." India has adopted a no-first-use nuclear policy, but the two nations have not resumed their strategic dialogue since their stalemate in Kashmir reached flash-point levels.

In any event, both India and Pakistan have had small but significant nuclear programs for the past two to three decades, and neither state is a signatory to the Nuclear Nonproliferation Treaty. India tested five nuclear devices in 1998 and may possess enough weapons-grade plutonium for forty to ninety nuclear weapons. Its Agni-2 ballistic missile is capable of striking Pakistan and southwestern China. Pakistan similarly tested five or six nuclear devices in 1998, and may possess enough weapons-grade uranium for twenty to forty nuclear weapons. Its Ghauri-2 ballistic missile is capable of striking anywhere in India. India, with a far larger population and a much greater Gross Domestic Product, spends more than $14 billion annually for its defense budget, approximately 3 percent of its GDP. Pakistan spends around $4 billion annually on defense, approximately 6 to 7 percent of its GDP.

NMD, by potentially inducing China to increase its nuclear capacity, would put pressure on India; and by its abrogation of the ABM Treaty, it would thwart Indian adherence to the Non-Proliferation and Comprehensive Test Ban treaties, neither of which India has yet signed. By provoking an arms build-up in India, NMD would put pressure on Pakistan. Neither country sees NMD to be in its national interest.

## OPPOSITION IN EUROPE

All of America's allies in Europe oppose the system. At the Group of Eight meeting of industrialized countries in Okinawa in July 2000, the European states warned that National Missile Defense would lead to a new round of the arms race and a challenge to international peace and stability. They particularly fear Chinese reaction to missile defense, as well as the abrogation of the ABM Treaty. No European nation has asked to join the system; only Australia has expressed support for it. NATO officials are concerned that the deployment of NMD will "decouple" the United States from Europe, which will not share the geopolitical or military protection of an anti-missile shield. German Foreign Minister Joschka Fischer remarked in 1999 that missile defense could lead to "split security standards within the Alliance," a situation wherein one ally is safer than the rest. Many Europeans fear this would lead either to the United States disengaging from Europe or becoming more inclined to intervene unilaterally and preemptively. Europeans would be at greater risk in both scenarios.

The Europeans are particularly concerned with any weakening—let alone abrogation—of the ABM Treaty. The European states may not be part of the treaty but they certainly have benefitted—along with the Chinese—from the curbs on anti-missile defenses. The limited strategic systems in Britain and France are far more lethal in an environment without strategic defense. Abrogation of the treaty also would significantly weaken the delicate fabric of arms control, which will be discussed in the next chapter. The French are particularly concerned with the precedent of the United States walking away from an international agreement. The political director of the French Foreign Ministry, Ambassador Gerard Errera, suggested that, if the United States was prepared to abrogate the ABM Treaty, then Washington must be prepared for the reality that other countries could abandon multilateral arms control regimes such as the Non-Proliferation Treaty. This attitude in Europe became more prevalent after the U.S. Senate refused to ratify the Comprehensive Test Ban Treaty.

European states have numerous concerns with NMD. They particularly fear that such a system will spark a renewed nuclear arms race and destabilize international security. They are concerned that any abrogation or even reinterpretation of the ABM Treaty will lead

Russia to withdraw from such arms control treaties as the Intermediate-Range Nuclear Forces Treaty or START, as they have warned. They also anticipate that Russia will divert resources from economic development to enhance its defense spending, and that increased military investment at this time would weaken Russia's economic capacity. There is a delicate political issue that will involve Europe as well, since NMD presumably would require the use of radar facilities in England and Greenland, a Danish territory. Acquiescence to the use of such radars would implicate these states in the operation of a system from which they would derive no benefit. For these reasons, German Chancellor Gerhard Schroder and Foreign Minister Joschka Fischer asked President Clinton to take European sensitivities into account before he made any decision on deployment. They had also suggested to their European allies that they develop a joint position on this controversial subject.

France and Britain expressed their reservations about NMD at the review of the Nuclear Nonproliferation Treaty in April and May 2000. Britain stated that the U.S. position on NMD and amendment of the ABM Treaty "should be addressed bilaterally with the Russians," and indicated that London continued to value the treaty. France also declared that it was "anxious to avoid any challenges to the treaty liable to bring about a breakdown of strategic equilibrium and to restart the arms race."

The European Union (EU) has taken a stand against NMD, declaring its unconditional opposition to the deployment of such a system because of its disruptive impact on arms control and strategic stability. A strong position would suggest that the EU hopes to influence the United States, perhaps reining in Washington's turn to unilateralism in its foreign policy. The EU also is calling for the preservation of the ABM Treaty and suggesting that the United States delay its decision on deployment to allow time for negotiations with Russia. A common European position against NMD would strengthen the credibility of the European Union to advance its own security interests. Thus far, it has resorted to general diplomatic language that expresses a desire to see international security preserved, for arms control treaties to be respected, and for the concerns of the allies to be weighed in the balance.

Clinton's Secretary of Defense William Cohen acknowledged that the United States needs the support of its European allies for a national missile defense, and that the allies must be convinced that

Washington has "at least tried to work it out with the Russians." Without radars in England and Greenland, the United States would not be able to see the missiles coming. U.S. interceptors, in the words of Cohen, would then "not be worth very much."

## THE NORTH KOREAN ANGLE

The specific policy rationalization for NMD is the need for a defense against the future strategic missile program of such "rogue states" as North Korea. As we have indicated (see Chapter Four), this is a ludicrous position. Given that ballistic missiles are inappropriate as terror weapons, and could only rain destruction on their sender, we must ask what purpose such a weapon could have for North Korea. Any state that develops strategic weapons is doing so to develop a tool of geopolitical strategy, not state terrorism. It is almost certain that Pyongyang only perceives its missile inventory as a device for altering the U.S. calculation of the costs and benefits of interfering in the Korean peninsula to challenge North Korean interests. Former Secretary of Defense Harold Brown even suggested that the United States would gain more protection from "rogue state" threats by beefing up the U.S. customs service than by deploying a national missile defense.

Second, as noted earlier, the United States is focusing on North Korea as the *raison d'être* for NMD at the very time that Pyongyang is moderating its policies, improving its relations with South Korea and Japan, and looking for ways to end its modest strategic programs. North and South Korea promised in the summer of 2000 to end a half-century of Cold War hostility, and Pyongyang is establishing diplomatic relations with such Western nations as Canada and Italy. China and Russia are implicitly cooperating to end North Korea's isolation, and the United States has been on the outside looking in. Moscow is doing so to build ties with countries that are out of favor with the United States, such as Iraq, Iran, and Libya. Beijing is doing so to increase its political influence in the region. Both Moscow and Beijing are trying to undercut the "rogue state" rationale behind Washington's plans for NMD, as well as the geostrategic rationale for the 37,000 American troops stationed in South Korea.

In addition to significant political and diplomatic moves, Pyongyang has not tested any of its missiles since 1998, when it unwisely test-fired its Taepo-Dong ballistic missile over Japan. In September

1999, Pyongyang pledged to halt further testing of long-range missiles. If North Korea does not flight-test the Taepo-Dong-2, which is believed to have a range of 2,500 to 3,700 miles, and, if Pyongyang can be convinced not to export missiles or related technology, the most likely source of an additional ICBM threat to the United States would be eliminated.

As noted in Chapter Four, during a summit meeting with Russian President Putin in July 2000, North Korean leader Kim Jong Il indicated that Pyongyang was prepared to end its missile program if it received international assistance in launching space satellites. The United States has suggested that, if the launch capability was outside the territory of North Korea, then Washington might agree. In any event, it appears that North Korea is looking for ways to become more conciliatory in the international arena, and that the United States is quickly losing its justification for a national missile defense. It would be particularly ironic if it turns out that Putin, the first Russian leader ever to visit Pyongyang, carried the diplomatic message that broke the nuclear stalemate on the Korean peninsula.

Third, the rush to develop a missile defense against North Korea is driven by a worst-case, politicized intelligence estimate that Pyongyang could develop a missile capable of striking parts of the United States by 2005. Satellite photography of the North Korean test facilities reveals a primitive missile program that is not capable of sustaining multiple launches of missiles. The Taepo-Dong missiles would have to make considerable progress in propulsion, guidance, and re-entry vehicle technology. Finally, Pyongyang would have to manufacture a nuclear warhead small enough and sturdy enough to fit on the tip of its missiles. There is no evidence that North Korea has mastered these techniques, only speculation that it might be possible.

From such speculation follows the argument that, if an anti-missile system is to be ready in Alaska by 2005, then work must begin by 2001 on a high-power radar station on a remote Aleutian island where weather conditions limit building activity. President Clinton's decision in September 2000 to delay preparatory work on a new radar for the system in Alaska will prevent the United States from meeting this schedule. Testing will continue, but now it will be up to President George W. Bush to decide whether the United States really needs missile defenses and, if so, what kind.

## NMD AND THE INTERNATIONAL MEDIA

The international press has been virtually unanimous in denouncing U.S. plans for national missile defense. The liberal *Guardian* of London, for instance, has repeatedly referred to the system as "fundamentally dotty." The test failure in the NMD program, which took place in July 2000, was headline news overseas, with articles indicating that leading NATO states, Russia, China, and Japan were breathing a cautious sigh of relief and hoping that it would spell the end of plans to proceed with NMD. The independent *Financial Times* termed the failure "opportune" and expressed hope that the United States would "work harder on alternative political means of dealing with the threat posed by the spread of long-range missile technology."

Numerous foreign newspapers have argued that the ABM Treaty should block development of an NMD system. Moscow's reformist *Izvestia*, for one, gloated that "it looks as if the Russians were right when they warned that ABM was not going to work." The centrist *Le Figaro* in Paris stated that any installation of NMD would "violate the 1972 ABM treaty on which rests the fragile balance of today." Even the right-of-center *Frankfurter Allgemeine* recorded that the system would "serve not just military ends, but first and foremost American domestic policies."

The international press has been particularly critical of the U.S. discussion to reinterpret the ABM Treaty in order to allow the beginning of construction of the system in Alaska. Munich's centrist *Sueddeutsche Zeitung* credited President Clinton with "turning U.S. foreign diplomacy into a field of rubble." Even before the test failure, foreign media took aim at the U.S. missile shield, with critical statements of NMD becoming a staple in editorial comment from a wide spectrum of papers in Europe, Asia, and South America. Since the State Department has stopped referring to "rogue states," many newspapers in Europe, including the centrist *Der Tagesspiegel* of Berlin; the right-of-center, business-oriented *Financial Times Deutschland* of Hamburg; and *L'Unita* of Rome have asked: "If there are no longer rogue states, then why NMD?" *L'Unita* asked Secretary of Defense Cohen that, if Secretary of State Madeleine Albright had dropped the reference to rogue states, then why did the Department of Defense continue to use it?

## IMPLICATIONS OF AN NMD SYSTEM

On balance, any decision to deploy NMD at any level will have a domino effect in U.S. bilateral relations and in the international arena. At the very least, U.S. deployment will lead to Russian and Chinese steps to increase their strategic offensive inventories. Any Chinese step to increase its nuclear inventories will lead directly to an Indian decision to match Beijing. Pakistan will match India. As part of this process, there will be a general breakdown or fissuring of the counterproliferation process, as the United States loses any credibility that it may have had as the leader of the nonproliferation regime for the past three decades.

In addition to significant increases in the nuclear inventories of the current strategic powers such as Russia, China, India, and Pakistan, there will be proliferation efforts that will help the "nonnuclears" to attain their own strategic forces. Iraq, Iran, and North Korea would obviously benefit from a renewed competition to build strategic forces. Egypt and Libya may reenter the nuclear competition. Israel, which already has about 200 nuclear weapons or "devices," would not stand by idly.

The abrogation of the ABM treaty and the deterioration of the nonproliferation and arms control regime go together. Also, European leaders have warned that any U.S. decision to deploy NMD would "decouple" the U.S. and European deterrence strategies and undermine the concept of "shared risk" that has held NATO together since the end of World War II. It is obvious that the security architecture of the Cold War and post–Cold War eras will have suffered a major defeat, and it is uncertain what institutions will replace the old ones, and how they will function.

While it is still an option, U.S. policy makers should consider the use of NMD as a bargaining chip, even if only as a bluff, as former national security advisor Robert McFarland and strategic arms negotiator Paul Nitze conceived "Star Wars" in 1983 (see Chapter One). For example, if the United States were to forego an NMD system in return for further reductions of strategic weapons by Russia, then there is greater likelihood that China would consider limitations on its own programs. North Korea's indications that it may give up its ballistic missile program in exchange for international help with "peaceful space research" may point to Pyongyang's willingness to seek a conciliatory approach to the issue of national missile defense.

Indeed, there is a need to examine the possibility of a reverse domino effect that would begin with an end to U.S. plans for a national missile defense. A conciliatory U.S. step on national missile defense could be used to invigorate counterproliferation policies toward China. Any sign of Chinese restraint could lead, in turn, to India's willingness to limit its own strategic programs. India and Pakistan, already trying to put the Kashmir issue on the back burner, could resume their own strategic dialogue to limit their nuclear programs. Finally, Iran and Iraq might even find it difficult to locate the technology for their own secret programs if such suppliers as China and North Korea showed genuine interest in counterproliferation policy. In any event, missile defenses or the absence of such defenses will play a major role in the configuration of the next nuclear era.

## NOTE

1. It is interesting to note that during the Cold War, the Soviet Union wanted these nuclear forces withdrawn from Europe. Their purpose, during that era, at least from the European perspective, was to couple two U.S. strategic forces by being a "tripwire." The idea was that these weapons would have to be used early during a Warsaw Pact attack, and the resulting nuclear detonations in the Soviet homeland would lead to an all out nuclear exchange involving U.S.-based nuclear forces. In principle, this brought Western Europe under the U.S. strategic nuclear umbrella.

## RESOURCES

Lawrence Freedman, *The Evolution of National Strategy* (Macmillan Press, 1983), and John Newhouse, *War and Peace in the Nuclear Age* (Alfred A. Knopf, 1989), are excellent sources on geopolitical implications of nuclear policy. See also Raymond L. Garthoff, *The Great Transition: American-Soviet Relations and the End of the Cold War* (Brookings Institution, 1994), and Frances Fitzgerald, *Way Out There in the Blue: Reagan, Star Wars and the End of the Cold War* (Simon & Schuster, 2000).

While the periodical literature is vast, the following articles have been drawn upon specifically for this chapter: George Lewis, Lisbeth Gronlund, and David Wright, "National Missile Defense: An Indefensible System," *Foreign Policy*, Winter 1999–2000; Joseph Cirincione, "The Asian Nuclear Reaction Chain," *Foreign Policy*, Spring 2000; Bruce W. MacDonald, "Falling Star: SDI's Troubled Seventh Year," *Arms Control Today*, September 1990; and Lawyers Alliance for World Security, *White Paper on National Missile*

*Defense*, Spring 2000. This latter pamphlet can be secured by writing the organization at 1901 Pennsylvania Avenue NW, Suite 201, Washington, DC 20036, or by E-mail at *disarmament@lawscns.org*. See also Charles Ferguson, "Sparking a Buildup: U.S. Missile Defense and China's Nuclear Arsenal," *Arms Control Today*, March 2000; Francois Heisbourg et al., "International Perspectives on National Missile Defense," *The Washington Quarterly*, Summer 2000; and Stephen W. Young, "Pushing the Limits: The Decision on National Missile Defense," A Report Sponsored by the Coalition to Reduce Nuclear Dangers and the Council for a Livable World Education Fund, April 2000.

This chapter, like others in the book, relies heavily on the thorough chronicling of NMD developments in the *New York Times, Washington Post, Financial Times*, and other newspapers.

## Chapter Eight

# Arms Control and Policy Alternatives

Arms control and disarmament did not emerge as major goals of U.S. foreign policy until after World War II and the widespread U.S. and Soviet deployment of nuclear missiles. President John F. Kennedy gave a huge boost to the importance of arms control in the nuclear era with his creation of the Arms Control and Disarmament Agency in 1961 and the negotiation of two major arms control agreements with the Soviet Union in the wake of the Cuban missile crisis of 1962. The first, the Hot Line Agreement, established a direct communications link between the world's only nuclear powers during times of crisis. The second, the 1963 Limited Test Ban Treaty, banned nuclear weapons tests in the atmosphere, outer space, and underwater. The success of the Limited Test Ban led directly to the 1968 Nonproliferation Treaty, which committed states that had not exploded a nuclear device to forfeit the right to build or use nuclear weapons and obligated nuclear weapons states to eliminate their own weapons. The Limited Test Ban Treaty was strengthened in 1974, when Washington and Moscow concluded a Threshold Test Ban Treaty to limit the size of weapons being tested underground.

In the 1960s, the United States and the Soviet Union also agreed to a ban on placing nuclear and other weapons of mass destruction in space. The Soviets had wanted such a ban in the 1950s, but the United States, arguing that offensive strategic ballistic missiles transit space during their flight trajectory, had insisted that a comprehensive agreement on intercontinental missiles would be required. They achieved such an agreement in 1963 in the form of a jointly sponsored U.N. General Assembly resolution and parallel national declarations of intent. These documents were converted into a treaty obligation in the Outer Space Treaty in 1967.

Détente in the 1970s between the two major nuclear powers—the United States and the Soviet Union—led to a series of arms control agreements designed to lessen the uncertainty of the nuclear era. In 1971, President Richard M. Nixon and Soviet leader Leonid Brezhnev completed the Accidental Measures Agreement to reduce the risk of nuclear war. The following year, the superpowers concluded both the Strategic Arms Limitations Talks Treaty (SALT), to impose caps on the future development of offensive strategic nuclear systems, and the Anti-Ballistic Missile Treaty, to impose strict limits on current and future strategic defensive capabilities. The ABM Treaty marked a major battle inside the Pentagon, with Secretary of Defense Robert McNamara and Deputy Secretary of Defense Cyrus Vance taking on the Joint Chiefs of Staff and a few congressional barons who strongly favored missile defense.

The next major round of Soviet-American disarmament agreements began in the mid-1980s, when the two sides agreed to jointly staff nuclear risk reduction centers and to remove all of their intermediate-range missile systems from Europe. These agreements were followed by the treaty on Conventional Forces in Europe (CFE) in 1990, which provided for deep reductions and significant restructuring of all East-West military forces between the Atlantic and the Urals. The CFE Treaty prescribed much greater troop reductions for the Soviets than for the West and presented the United States with a decided military advantage in Europe. The discrepancy did not pose a problem of real military significance to the Soviet Union, but the perception of a one-sided Soviet retreat contributed to Mikhail Gorbachev's political problems, which led to his removal from the Kremlin in a "constitutional" *coup d'état* in December 1991.

Two Strategic Arms Reduction Treaties (START) in the early 1990s significantly reduced strategic missiles and banned multiple independently targeted re-entry vehicles (MIRVs). START I, signed in July 1991, reduced the number of strategic nuclear warheads from approximately 10,000 to 6,000 for each side over a seven-year period. The totals excluded sea-launched cruise missiles, which were limited to 880 for each side by a separate agreement. A follow-on agreement removed cruise missiles with a range in excess of 600 kilometers from operational deployment, and all nuclear weapons from surface ships. START II, signed in January 1993, further reduced strategic nuclear warheads to 3,500 for each side, and removed multiple warhead land-based ballistic missiles. A framework for START III, signed in 1997, endorsed additional reductions to 2,000 to 2,500 warheads.

## BAN ON MISSILE DEFENSE FOSTERS ARMS CONTROL

The key to reducing strategic offensive weapons has been the continuing Russian-American acceptance of a ban on national missile defenses based on the realization by the United States and the Soviet Union that NMD is not feasible and that development of such systems would be both expensive and destabilizing. Ironically, it was the Soviets who originally were determined to continue with missile defense. "Defense is moral, offense is immoral," Soviet Premier Aleksei Kosygin said to Secretary of Defense McNamara in 1967 at the Glassboro Summit.

Reason prevailed, however. The Soviets soon realized that their primitive anti-ballistic missile system around Moscow would be ineffective and that the United States, working from a wider and deeper technological base, just might build a national system that worked. Moscow's realization that proceeding with a national defensive system would end any chance for limiting offensive systems coincided with the U.S. breakthrough on the development of MIRVs, which promised another cycle of the arms race. Since President Lyndon B. Johnson was a lame duck weakened by the Vietnam War, the actual agreement to limit anti-ballistic missiles had to await the election of a new president. The Soviets, who had not been ready to negotiate an anti-ballistic missile treaty in 1967 at Glassboro, had to wait another five years.

The Anti-Ballistic Missile Treaty of 1972 remains the cornerstone of today's arms control regime. As understood in both Washington and Moscow, nationwide defensive deployments would lead to ever larger and more sophisticated offensive systems on both sides as well as in the nuclear inventories of China, Britain, and France. The deployment of a national missile defense at virtually any level would destroy the institutional framework for preventing the proliferation of nuclear weapons and nuclear technology. International agreements such as the Non-Proliferation Treaty and international institutions such as the International Atomic Energy Agency have frustrated the efforts of bomb advocates in the near-nuclear weapons states. More than a dozen nations, including Argentina, Brazil, Libya, Egypt, and South Africa, have started down the path of nuclear weapons, only to stop and reverse course. The entire continent of South America, in accord with the Treaty of Tlatelolco, has declared itself nuclear-free; the nations of the South Pacific have made the same decision. France has reduced its nuclear testing program due to domestic and international opposition. Abrogation of the Anti-Ballistic Missile Treaty and deployment of a national missile defense could reopen the debate.

Former President Clinton's speech on September 1, 2000, which acknowledged the Anti-Ballistic Missile Treaty as the cornerstone of strategic stability and removed the missile defense decision from the election-year agenda, also pointed to the danger from Russia's strategic arsenal. The tragic loss of the Russian strategic submarine *Kursk* and its crew of 118 sailors several weeks before Clinton's speech dramatically called attention to Moscow's inability to control its nuclear technology. Like the Chernobyl disaster in 1986, the *Kursk* disaster begged questions about the ability of the Russian military to operate sophisticated technology, and the world's vulnerability to the weakness and inadequacy of the Russian Federation. Thousands of nuclear weapons in Russia may be vulnerable to theft, and the bureaucratic bungling that accompanied the loss of the *Kursk* does not lead to confidence. After a previous military disaster, Russian former Prime Minister Viktor Chernomyrdin noted: "We hoped for the best, but things turned out as usual."

## EFFECTS OF NMD

Fortunately, Clinton recognized that any U.S. deployment of a national missile defense system and abrogation of the Anti-Ballistic Missile Treaty would harm the United States' strategic position and compromise its counterproliferation strategy. A national system would violate both the letter and spirit of the Anti-Ballistic Missile Treaty, ending the nuclear deterrence and arms control policies that the United States has pursued for over thirty years. The precedent of abrogating an international agreement would undermine American credibility in the international arena and allow Russia to withdraw from current treaties that limit strategic offensive weapons. Russian ratification of START II, for example, explicitly stated that Moscow could withdraw from that treaty if the United States were to abrogate the ABM Treaty.

Clinton's decision to defer the decision on National Missile Defense was greeted in the international community, including leading NATO countries as well as Russia, China, and Japan, as a "wise" and "immensely welcome" move. While Clinton merely kicked the dossier on national missile defense into his successor's in-basket, international leaders credited him with making the world a safer place. Many foreign editorials, however, warned that Clinton's "postponement, not cancellation" grants no more than a "temporary reprieve," and that the "debate in the United States is not whether but when and in what form to deploy missile defense."

As we have seen, the Central Intelligence Agency had complicated the decision-making process in 1999 when it issued a National Intelligence Estimate ("Foreign Missile Developments and the Ballistic Missile Threat to the United States") that argued in favor of an increased strategic threat from so-called rogue states. However, in the summer of 2000, the White House received another National Intelligence Estimate ("Foreign Responses to U.S. National Missile Defense Deployment") that warned of a new arms race with Russia and China if the United States deployed even a limited defensive system. For the first time, the CIA presented the White House with the downside of the deployment of a national missile defense. The still-classified estimate concluded that China's response to national missile defense would include the development of both mobile and multiple-warhead missiles, as well as the deployment of as many as 200 nuclear warheads. The study also anticipated a Russian return to the deployment of multiple warheads, and a Russian withdrawal from "an array of arms control treaties."

President Clinton had several major arms control objectives *vis-à-vis* Russia: the need to settle the issue of national missile defense, to reduce strategic offensive weapons, and to protect the Anti-Ballistic Missile Treaty. This followed on the dismantling of nuclear weapons systems in non-Russian republics of the former Soviet Union— Ukraine, Belarus, and Kazakhstan—which the president cited in his speech. All the strategic missile systems in these three republics have been destroyed or dismantled; the only remaining strategic system, the TU-95 strategic bomber, is being dismantled in Ukraine. Some of this work was underwritten by the Nunn-Lugar Bill (the Cooperative Threat Reduction Act) of 1992, which used Department of Defense appropriations to dismantle the former Soviet arsenal and thus end the problem of "loose nukes" in the former non-Russian Soviet republics. Earlier negotiations between the United States and the former Soviet Union eliminated theater nuclear systems deployed in Central Europe.

Discussions between the United States and Russia have focused on a third Strategic Arms Reduction Talks Treaty, with the Russians willing to reduce to 1,000 to 1,500 strategic warheads and the United States holding firm at 2,000 to 2,500. The two sides will have to agree on a number and then decide how to distribute these warheads among existing categories of weapons. Then the two sides must determine the relationship between the new strategic inventory and national missile defense. This dialogue will go a long way toward defining the strategic relationship between the United States and Russia over the next five to ten years.

## MILITARIZATION OF FOREIGN POLICY

Until Clinton's decision to defer any deployment of a national missile defense, his administration's tendency to defer to the policy interests of certain groups in the Pentagon and meet the criticisms of the Republican right wing had limited its ability to conduct a coherent foreign policy. Although the collapse of the Berlin Wall ended the Cold War and placed the United States in an unprecedented position of preeminence, two administrations—one Republican, the other Democratic—conducted national security policies without a strategic framework adequate to the challenges of the post–Cold War era. President George Bush and his national security advisor, General Brent Scowcroft, referred to a "new world order," but this vacuous phrase provided no guidance for the conduct of foreign policy. President Clinton and his secretary of state, Madeleine Albright, designated the United States the "indispensable nation," revealing the arrogance of a global power without a military rival.

As Professor Stephen Walt wrote in *The National Interest*, "military superiority is a good thing, but too much of a good thing is usually unhealthy." In the case of President Clinton's foreign policy, military superiority had led to the policy of unilateralism (see Chapter Three), which has often reflected the interests of some in the uniformed military and the political instincts of the Republican opposition. As we have seen, Clinton retreated from a number of international agreements or covenants that both groups opposed, including measures on arms control and international criminal law.

Despite the absence of a strategic threat and the presence of international opposition, the United States has been headed towards deployment of a national ballistic missile defense, a clearly unnecessary concession to the right wing of the Republican party and the military-industrial complex. As in the case of the Comprehensive Test Ban Treaty, the Clinton administration failed to explain the facts to the American people and only deferred the decision to deploy national missile defense at the last possible moment.

If the decision is made to go ahead in the current administration of George W. Bush, it will involve the destruction of the Anti-Ballistic Missile Treaty, the cornerstone of U.S. deterrence for the past thirty years; the alienation of Russia and China from the arms control process; the opposition of America's NATO allies; and the end of U.S. leadership to stop proliferation of nuclear weapons. National missile defense and continued rejection of the Comprehensive Test Ban Treaty would destabilize American national security policy and greatly increase American defense spending.

To summarize, deployment of national missile defense and the abrogation of the Anti-Ballistic Missile Treaty would register a net decrease in U.S. security, exchanging an inadequate defense for the abrogation of two important treaties and the ensuing instability. As we have seen, tests indicate that the system is not workable. It cannot distinguish between real and fake targets; it can be underflown by short-range ballistic and cruise missiles; it cannot protect against "submunitions" designed to disperse chemical and biological agents, and it would be vulnerable to unsophisticated countermeasures. Since a national missile defense system could never be tested in battlefield conditions, any shortcomings would not become apparent until it was too late. Finally, as a counter to U.S. strategic defenses, it would lead such states as Russia and China to augment their strategic offensive programs with the further complications of unstable launch on warning command and control procedures. National missile defense at any level would undercut U.S. efforts to counter the proliferation of strategic weaponry, thus jeopardizing strategic stability.

## ALTERNATIVES TO NMD

Instead of national missile defense, the United States should be looking for ways to reduce its nuclear inventory and guarantee the command and control of nuclear weapons elsewhere. The problem is a serious one because large Russian and American nuclear arsenals act as a goad to proliferation. Indian Foreign Minister Jaswant Singh, for example, has referred to the Russian and American arsenals as a "nuclear paradigm" emulated by other countries. As we have noted (see Chapter Four), several dozen nations have the capacity to build nuclear weapons.

One way to achieve strategic stability and perhaps increase the opportunities for counterproliferation would be to significantly reduce the 2,200 strategic weapons that the United States now has on alert. Admiral Stansfield Turner, former director of the Central Intelligence Agency, advocates the creation of a "strategic escrow"; he suggests removing the warheads from 1,000 nuclear missiles and placing them in designated storage areas some distance from their launchers. The remaining alert weapons would still be numerous enough to prevent the instability associated with very low numbers. This step would require neither Senate approval nor the tortuous negotiations of reductions in strategic arsenals.

Implementation of a "strategic escrow" would be designed to get Russia to take similar steps and to re-energize the disarmament process. Such a step would be more meaningful than detargeting and dealerting missiles because these steps can be reversed in minutes or hours. Verification of a strategic escrow would be an easy matter as well, requiring only observers at each storage site. A more radical procedure would involve the use of separate storage sites for such components as guidance sets separated from their weapons, or plutonium pits from their warheads.

Turner's idea would be particularly meaningful if applied to land-based missiles, as these must be launched on warning of an attack if they are to survive. In this way, the strategic escrow idea could cut nuclear arms, yet at the same time it would not decrease the stability presently achieved through the ability to wait until actual nuclear detonations occur on U.S. territory confirming an attack. Land-based missiles must be launched on warning; the Trident and the bomber force, if properly operated, can wait.

The United States is in a strong position to accept the unofficial Russian proposal to reduce its nuclear inventory to 1,500 strategic weapons and still maintain a credible deterrent. China believes that it can achieve nuclear deterrence with no more than 20 intercontinental missiles; the United States should be able to do so with 1,500.

But the U.S. Joint Chiefs of Staff believe we must maintain 2,500 strategic weapons. The U.S. strategic war plan (the single integrated operational plan, or SIOP) currently has more than 2,200 strategic targets in the Russian Federation, more targets than there were in the Russian Republic before the dissolution of the Soviet Union. These figures indicate that the Pentagon still presumes a series of nuclear exchanges based on the exceptionally deep rivalries and differences of the Cold War. Admiral Richard W. Mies, Commander-in-Chief, U.S. Strategic Command, told a congressional committee in June 2000, "These forces represent our nation's ultimate insurance policy. Nuclear weapons help keep the cold war cold." The more things change, the more they stay the same.

The Senate made the possibility of unilateral cuts more possible by voting in June 2000 to allow the president to reduce the U.S. nuclear arsenal, but only after a nuclear posture review by the Pentagon. The posture review was designed to make sure that President Clinton did not have the opportunity to accomplish such a reduction, but that his successor would have that opportunity.

Russian President Vladimir Putin is prepared to reduce Moscow's strategic arsenal unilaterally, regardless of U.S. actions. In the summer of 2000, he intervened in a debate between his defense minister, Igor Sergeyev, and the chief of the general staff, Anatoly Kvashnin. Sergeyev, a former head of the Strategic Rocket Forces, has favored the modernization of Russian strategic forces; Kvashnin, an army officer, believes that conventional forces need to be modernized and that unilateral strategic cutbacks would help to bankroll conventional force modernization. In view of the current problems that confront Russia—ethnic violence, terrorism, drug operations, and peacekeeping—Kvashnin's argument is a sound one. In any event, the Russian military appears to support Putin's proposal to cut back to 1,000 strategic warheads, but presumably it would favor doing so as part of negotiations and not as a unilateral action.

Putin favors cooperation with the United States in safeguarding Russia's nuclear facilities because of the Kremlin's concern with terrorism, particularly nuclear terrorism. In the wake of the *Kursk* tragedy, some Russian officials briefly encouraged the notion that Chechen terrorism may have been involved in the blast on the nuclear submarine that led to the loss of 118 lives. In any event, Russian and American diplomats now have an opportunity to help prevent terrorist theft of Russian nuclear weapons and weapons-grade nuclear materials. The nuclear powers could agree that the United States purchase all the nuclear weapons material that Russia is prepared to sell. In addition to highly enriched uranium purchases, the United States should buy all available Russian plutonium, although it currently has no commercial use. The United States, using the Nunn-Lugar program, should cooperate with Russia by funding the removal of potential bomb material from vulnerable sites in Russia to secure facilities. These deals should be accompanied by Russia's agreement not to produce additional nuclear materials.

Along with the creation of a strategic escrow, the United States should abandon its launch-on-warning doctrine and its doctrine to be the first to employ nuclear weapons under certain circumstances. Currently, U.S. strategic forces are on an alert status that is comparable to the Cold War level. The risk of keeping much of its nuclear inventory on high alert was put to the test in the last months of the Carter administration. As reported by former CIA director Robert M. Gates, Carter's assistant for national security, Zbigniew Brzezinski, received a call from a staff officer at 2:26 A.M. on June 3, 1980. The officer reported that the U.S. warning system was predicting a nuclear attack of 220 missiles on the United States. Brzezinski was convinced we had to retaliate, but knew that the president's decision time for ordering retaliation was from three to seven minutes after a Soviet launch, and wanted a confirmation call from the staff officer.

Shortly after, Brzezinski received a second call and was told that warning indicators were now pointing to an all-out attack of 2,220 missiles. U.S. bomber crews were now manning their aircraft, and the Pacific Command's airborne command post had taken off. One minute before his call to the president, Brzezinski received a third call that informed him that only one of our warning stations had reported the impending attack, suggesting that someone had mistakenly put military exercise tapes into the computer system. The crisis came and went in a matter of minutes, but the implementation of a U.S. launch-on-warning doctrine would have brought nuclear devastation.

Russia experienced a similar episode in 1995 when it confused a NASA-funded research rocket for a NATO missile and feared that a nuclear attack was underway. The rocket was launched in January 1995 from a civilian research base on the Norwegian Arctic island of Andoya. A former CIA officer, Peter Pry, reported that the Russian military made all of the preparations for starting a nuclear war except the final decision to launch. President Boris Yeltsin had even reportedly consulted codes to be used when ordering a nuclear strike. The rocket never came near Russian territory and fell into the Arctic Ocean as planned.[1]

It is noteworthy that these early warning crises were resolved when it was confirmed that there was no strategic threat facing the United States and Russia. Strategic stability between the two major nuclear powers is now threatened because of the deterioration of Moscow's surveillance system. The United States has a series of sophisticated satellites, but most of Russia's early-warning satellites have either stopped functioning or have strayed from their assigned orbits. Russia currently has five early-warning satellites ready to be launched into space, but lacks the resources to launch them. It is estimated that $160 million is needed to complete the task; if the joint early-warning center planned for Moscow is to be effective, it is important that both sides have dependable satellite vehicles.

## NON-FIRST USE OF NUCLEAR WEAPONS

Several NATO allies of the United States want to renounce any first use of nuclear weapons, but the United States refuses to consider such a step despite the overwhelming superiority of both its conventional and its strategic deterrents. The United States has attempted to address the incentive for Third World countries to develop nuclear weapons to deter this country by offering, in connection with a UN Special Session on Disarmament in 1978, the assurance that the United States would "not use nuclear weapons against any non-nuclear weapons state party to the NPT (Non-Proliferation Treaty) or any comparable internationally binding commitment not to acquire nuclear explosive devices." However, this assurance does not apply "in the case of an attack on the United States, its territories or armed forces, or its allies, by such a state allied to a nuclear weapons state, or associated with a nuclear weapons state in carrying out or sustaining the attack." Consider such a guarantee from the Iraqi perspective when it was being militarily supplied by the Soviet Union. The Iraqis might well believe that the United States would consider a military supply relationship to be an alliance. Because the escape clause is so broad, the guarantee is unlikely to offer much assurance to any except the most pacific of states.

Bilateral negotiations with Third World countries could yield agreements by which the United States traded a no-first-use promise in exchange for assurances that the Third World country would not develop chemical or biological weapons. Bilateral no-first-use statements or agreements with Russia and China could soften the nuclear ambitions of both declared nuclear nations and even "undeclared" nuclear states such as India and Pakistan.[2] Russia actually had a long-standing no-first-use pledge until 1993, when it withdrew its unilateral statement out of concern that it might need tactical nuclear weapons to supplement its inadequate conventional forces.

China has consistently pledged no-first-use, but U.S. deployment of any national missile defense presumably would alter that doctrine. Unlike a treaty, no-first-use statements would not require extensive negotiation and ratification by the Senate.

A no-first-use pledge that included the United States, Russia, and China and perhaps Britain and France would make it easier to impose sanctions against any state that was a base for nuclear terrorists or that planned to use nuclear weapons. If the no-first-use states were to support an end to all economic and commercial activity with offending states, or to use conventional military force to enforce air and sea blockades, then there might be less of a threat from so-called rogue states. A reduced threat from these states would lessen the need for a national missile defense. A no-first-use pledge by the nuclear powers should be accompanied by increasing transparency for the weapons programs of the nonnuclear states, including inspection and provisions to control nuclear-related materials such as enriched uranium and plutonium.

Finally, the United States should finance and establish the Moscow-based Joint Center for the Exchange of Data from Early Warning Systems and Notification of Missile Launches. The Center was agreed to in 1997 at the Russian-American summit in Helsinki because of mutual concerns about the effectiveness and safety of Russian monitoring capabilities. The Center is supposed to open in June 2001, with a staff of fifteen to twenty Russians and the same number of Americans. Both American and Russian specialists believe that Russian early warning systems are dilapidated, unreliable, and unable to detect all launches. Moscow favors the establishment of the early warning center but some military officers, convinced that the Soviet Union was outnegotiated in the Intermediate-Range Nuclear Forces Treaty and the Strategic Arms Reduction Talks Treaty, fear that Washington would use the Center to obtain sensitive data on the gaps in Russian monitoring capabilities.

## THE DIPLOMATIC ROUTE TO COUNTERPROLIFERATION

Most arms control experts believe that multilateral diplomatic approaches are more effective in dealing with the nuclear ambitions of Iran, Iraq, and North Korea than the unilateral approach of the United States. These experts favor placing international inspectors in the key countries and endorsing intrusive on-site inspection to monitor the possibility of covert acquisition of nuclear weapons. The United Nations and the International Atomic Energy Agency could be used to manage the proliferation threat in the so-called rogue states, if the appropriate agreements could be negotiated and maintained. These agencies certainly have been more effective than the continued bombing of Iraqi military facilities, and their efforts are a model for the monitoring of strategic weapons programs in North Korea or Iran. As we have noted, with North Korea keeping its pledge to stop testing a ballistic missile capable of reaching the continental United States, with most worst-case estimates putting Pyongyang a decade away from deploying one, and with Pyongyang entering normalization talks with both South Korea and Japan, Washington is in a good position at this juncture to negotiate a ban on development, production, and export of Pyongyang's medium- and long-range missiles. Such a diplomatic solution would be far less risky and costly than deployment of a national missile defense.

## THE GEOPOLITICAL IMPLICATIONS OF NMD

As we have indicated, any U.S. decision to deploy national missile defense and to reinterpret or abrogate the Anti-Ballistic Missile Treaty will end the progress that has been achieved in arms control and disarmament in recent years. We have seen significant progress in denuclearizing the American and Russian strategic inventories beginning with the Intermediate-Range Nuclear Forces Treaty in 1989, which eliminated entire categories of intermediate-range weapons and the nuclear instability that these weapons introduced; then moving to Strategic Arms Reduction Talks I and II, which established significantly lower ceilings for strategic missiles and banned land-based multiple independently targeted re-entry vehicles. U.S. efforts to denuclearize the inventories of Belarus, Kazakhstan, and Ukraine have been successful; earlier, the governments of Argentina, Brazil and South Africa unilaterally renounced their nuclear weapons programs. The Agreed Framework between the United States and North Korea established a nuclear freeze in Pyongyang, and now the North Koreans are willing to discuss a further rollback of their nuclear inventory.

One of the toughest strategic problems in the arms control arena is the need to add India and Pakistan to the list of Non-Proliferation Treaty signatories. The Senate's failure to ratify the Comprehensive Test Ban Treaty dealt a major setback to the nuclear challenge from South Asia; if the United States actually moves away from the Anti-Ballistic Missile Treaty, it will become even more difficult to resolve this problem. It is ironic that as nuclear weapons become more superfluous in our basic military posture, the United States is taking the very steps that will make denuclearization and disarmament more difficult.

The deployment of national missile defense would complicate the most important problem that confronts the nonproliferation policy of the United States, namely the nuclear and missile threat from India and Pakistan. India has singled out the Chinese threat to justify its nuclear activities, although China has no apparent designs on Indian territory or resources. Pakistan, in turn, has used the Indian threat to justify its weapons programs and its rejection of the Non-Proliferation Treaty. Thus, both programs have a self-fulfilling logic, and both states indeed conducted nuclear tests in 1998. The U.S. deployment of a national missile defense presumably would lead to additional strategic programs in China, which in turn would trigger additional nuclear break-out activities in India and Pakistan. The continued Indian-Pakistani squabbling over the sovereignty of Kashmir will add to the military tensions and strategic activities of the two sides. It is difficult to imagine bringing these activities under control without extensive U.S. diplomatic intervention.

## THE ALTERNATIVE TO UNILATERALISM

The larger geopolitical issue is whether the United States will continue to follow a policy of unilateralism or pursue a policy of multilateralism. U.S. support for multilateralism in the diplomatic arena would enable Washington to establish the machinery and rules for international peacekeeping, counterproliferation, and avoidance of regional conflict. A more stable international system should be the goal; the sharing of U.S. power and influence is an acceptable price.

Multilateralism or "mutualism" recognizes that there is need for radical change in the international arena and that, as Hugh De Santis points out in the Winter 1998/1999 issue of *World Policy Journal*, "If no nation possesses the resources to solve or even manage the array of global problems that lie ahead," the United States must be part of an "interdependent community of nations that . . . rely on each other to satisfy their respective interests and goals." In the field of counterproliferation, such multilateral agreements as the Nuclear Nonproliferation Treaty (1968), the Comprehensive Test Ban Treaty, and the Missile Technology Control Regime have been effective in limiting the number of nuclear-capable states. This security architecture has led to some control over the development and transfer of nuclear technology, and has been a reminder to the nuclear powers of the need to reduce their nuclear inventories. Nevertheless, progress has been slow and, even if START II is fully implemented in 2003, the United States and Russia will have approximately the same number of nuclear warheads that they had at the time the Non-Proliferation Treaty was signed.

The collapse of the Soviet Union in 1991 gave the United States an unrivaled strategic position and great freedom of action, but Washington has squandered this position and the privileges that accompany it. The myth of American exceptionalism has dominated Washington's post–Cold War strategy. Washington has resorted to the language of the Cold War in dealing with Iran and Iraq ("dual containment") and with such weak and impoverished states as North Korea, Cuba, and Libya (the "rogue states"). This is the language of tutelage, not statesmanship. The expansion of NATO, the Senate's refusal to ratify the Comprehensive Test Ban Treaty, and the U.S. promotion of national missile defense are additional indicators of the United States deciding to force its way in the international community.

Diplomatic solutions to major problems will not be reached as long as the United States resorts to the military instrument. Ten years after the collapse of the Berlin Wall, the United States conducted a strategic bombing campaign against a European capital, and ten years after Desert Storm, it is still regularly bombing Iraqi targets. The Bush administration seems determined to spend at least $60 billion on building Ronald Reagan's space toy and thus reward the defense contractors who have lobbied for this boondoggle long and hard for the past two decades. Any promise of a green light for national missile defense and a red light for a Comprehensive Nuclear Test Ban points to another arms race in the near term. The United States often has demonstrated that "if the only tool in the toolbox is a hammer, then all of our problems will soon look like nails." Washington needs new tools.

## NOTES

1. Soviet military doctrine had long held that a possible design for launching an attack would be the conversion of an exercise simulating attack into a real attack. In 1983, NATO actually conducted an extensive exercise (*Able Archer*) that simulated nuclear release procedures, which caused genuine alarm in the Kremlin and the KGB. On the heels of the exercise, Soviet Defense Minister Marshal Dmitri Ustinov remarked that U.S. and NATO exercises are "characterized by vast scope and it becomes more and more difficult to distinguish them from the real deployment of armed forces for aggression." CIA director William Casey briefed President Ronald Reagan on the Kremlin's concern, and the president recorded in his memoirs that he was surprised to learn that the Soviet leaders were genuinely afraid of an American attack.

2. The declared nuclear states are China, France, Russia, United Kingdom, and the United States. The undeclared nuclear weapons states, with one or more nuclear weapons, are India, Israel, and Pakistan. The high-risk states, suspected of seeking a nuclear weapons capability, are Iran, Iraq Libya, and North Korea. The states that have abandoned their nuclear programs include Algeria, Argentina, Belarus, Brazil, Kazakhstan, South Africa, and Ukraine. Countries with the technical capacity to develop weapons but which have thus far abstained from doing so include Australia, Belgium, Canada, Finland, Germany, Italy, Japan, Mexico, Norway, South Korea, Sweden, Switzerland, and Taiwan.

## RESOURCES

A good historical source is John Newhouse, *War and Peace in the Nuclear Age* (Alfred A. Knopf, 1989). See also Stansfield Turner, *Caging the Nuclear Genie: An American Challenge for Global Security* (Westview Press, 1997), and Raymond L. Garthoff, *The Great Transition: American-Soviet Relations and the End of the Cold War* (The Brookings Institution, 1994). See Harold A. Feiveson, ed., *The Nuclear Turning Point: A Blueprint for Deep Cuts and De-Altering of Nuclear Weapons* (The Brookings Institution, 1999). For an alternative position on arms control, see Jonathan Schell, "The Folly of Arms Control," *Foreign Affairs*, September/October 2000. See also, Stephen Walt, "Too Much of a Good Thing," *The National Interest* 50 (Winter 1998): 38–46.

A Cold War perspective on intelligence can be found in Robert M. Gates, *Inside the Shadows: The Ultimate Insider's Story of Five Presidents and How They Won the Cold War* (Simon & Schuster, 1996). See also Ronald Reagan, *An American Life* (Simon & Schuster, 1990).

See also Leon V. Sigal, "Negotiating an End to North Korea's Missile-Making," *Arms Control Today*, June 2000; Scott Ritter, "The Case for Iraq's Qualitative Disarmament," *Arms Control Today*, June 2000; and Hugh De Santis, "Mutualism: An American Strategy for the Next Century," *World Policy Journal*, Winter 1998/1999.

# Appendix One

# Countermeasures

Countermeasures, or the use of decoys, chaff, and other such means of deception, are the Achilles' heel of every missile defense system ever proposed. These are not theoretical constructs; both the Soviet Union and the United States and its allies had large programs to develop and deploy countermeasures during the Cold War, and used them on selected ballistic missiles. They have been tested, and they work. Had the countermeasures volume of the Strategic Defense Initiative "Study on Eliminating the Threat Posed by Ballistic Missiles" not been marked "SECRET," so that it would have been available to the public in 1983, "Star Wars" would have had a very short life, and the country would have saved many billions of dollars. Hopefully, in the case of national missile defense, reason may yet prevail.

In evaluating the opposing technical claims made by supporters and opponents of national missile defense, the public's best hope is to use common sense, examine the available evidence, and look at where the vested interests lie. It is also important to distinguish between those claims that could, at least in principle, be achieved through additional technical development and those that violate basic physical principles. For example, as discussed in Chapter Five, Dr. Jacques Gansler's claim that an X-band radar is capable of measuring the mass of objects in the near vacuum of space violates a basic physical principle. No amount of technical development of radar, or any other remote sensor, will allow this to be done. The ability to distinguish between limitations of technology and those imposed by basic science is crucial to the discussion of countermeasures. The following discussion examines some of those scientific and technological limits.

When one asks the question "Will it work?" about any ballistic missile defense, it is imperative to answer with "Work against what?" Besides getting the technology to simply function as designed, the key problem for national missile defense is discrimination: the system must be able to differentiate between objects that are warheads and those that are decoys designed to fool the interceptor's sensors. To discriminate these objects from each other, the defense's exoatmospheric kill vehicle uses repeated observations with different sensor systems, which rely on different physical principles. In the case of the proposed National Missile Defense system, one sensor system uses visible light and at least two long infrared wavelengths to measure an object's temperature. A second system uses an X-band radar to measure the velocity of any attacking object and the size it appears to the radar, called its "cross section." Multiple sensors are designed to make it more difficult to create decoys that mimic the actual re-entry vehicle containing the warhead.

What makes countermeasures so damaging is that, despite such sophisticated sensing systems, the countermeasures do not have to be particularly sophisticated to fool them. As noted earlier, the "states of concern," which represent the "emerging threat," are fully capable of including effective countermeasures with their first intercontinental ballistic missile deployments. Indeed, the September 1999 National Intelligence Estimate warned that "countries developing ballistic missiles would also develop various responses to US theater and national defenses. . . . [T]hese countries could develop countermeasures . . . by the time they flight test their missiles." It also states that "Russia and China each have developed numerous countermeasures and probably are willing to sell the requisite technology."

Making a decoy that has the appearance of a re-entry vehicle containing a warhead is called "simulation." This may be less effective, and more costly, than making the re-entry vehicle look like a decoy. This is known as "anti-simulation."

Consider first the simulation approach. Here, one tries to deploy large numbers of decoys that are indistinguishable in appearance—from the warhead-containing re-entry vehicle—to the defensive system's sensors, but not necessarily to the human eye. The defense, while it may know about the re-entry vehicle's general characteristics, may not know its exact characteristics. Thus, if there is uncertainty as to whether the defense could possibly exploit some small observable difference between the re-entry vehicle and the decoys, one can make decoys that appear to have slightly different features from the re-entry vehicle and each other. Such an approach is known as "signature diversity." Simulation is a sort of cat-and-mouse game: one can always argue that better or more diverse sensors could discriminate the warhead, while more clever decoy designers could fool the sensors. A country not as technologically sophisticated as the United States would probably not choose this option.

Anti-simulation is another matter. A simple and effective example of anti-simulation is to use metallized balloons as decoys, and to enclose the re-entry vehicle containing the warhead in a similar balloon. Such a technique renders the National Missile Defense X-band radar useless since it cannot penetrate the thin metal coating of the balloon. The only remaining characteristic that could be used for discrimination is temperature, which can be dealt with in a variety of ways. These include controlling the temperature of the balloons to mimic the one containing the re-entry vehicle and warhead; using the signature diversity approach by giving each of the balloon decoys different temperatures; and cooling the re-entry vehicle.

Thermal interaction of the re-entry vehicle with the balloon must be controlled not only for equilibrium temperature but also for temperature rates of change and behavior in sunlight and in the earth's shadow. This is most easily achieved by reducing the amount of heat that can flow from the re-entry vehicle containing the warhead to the balloon's surface. If this is done, the thermal behavior of the warhead-enclosing balloon and all of the other balloon decoys will be identical. One way to achieve this is simply to vent the inflating gas and give the re-entry vehicle a polished silver surface finish. One can also use the signature diversity approach by varying the shape of the balloons, which in turn varies their equilibrium temperatures.

While the anti-simulation, metallized balloon countermeasure is conceptually simple, a subtlety should be mentioned. The interaction of the re-entry vehicle containing the warhead and an enclosing balloon must be controlled so as to prevent changes in balloon shape or motion that could be used to discriminate it from other balloon decoys. This can be done. The details, however, depend on the warhead's exact motion, for example, whether it is spinning or tumbling; whether the warhead's re-entry vehicle is attached to the balloon; and if so, how.

Once the re-entry vehicle containing the warhead is placed in a properly designed metallized balloon, one is no longer dealing with a cat-and-mouse game. No amount of technological development of sensors or their analysis software will allow the interceptor to discriminate a warhead-containing balloon from a decoy. One cannot extract information for such a decision where there is none. The signatures of the two do not differ. This is basic science, not technology.

How about the cost of countermeasures? This is a tricky question. The really large costs have to do with flight tests; but flight tests for countermeasures are generally piggy-backed on re-entry vehicle tests; so one should really talk about incremental costs, and these are generally relatively small. Developmental costs for simple countermeasures are also relatively small. Another measure of cost is to compare the weight of re-entry vehicles and their warheads with that associated with countermeasures and their inflating (if balloon or inflatable decoy countermeasures are used) and deployment mechanisms. Since the cost of launching an intercontinental missile is comparable to the cost of a commercial space launch to place a weight similar to the re-entry vehicles in orbit, this gives a reasonable quantitative estimate. In general, the costs for countermeasures are hundreds of times less than those for actual warheads containing re-entry vehicles.

Any country that could flight test an intercontinental ballistic missile will be able to develop numerous countermeasures to penetrate a missile defense system. Countries attempting to develop medium- or long-range missiles would not, however, have to rely on the purchase or transfer of countermeasure technology. The 1999 NIE lists eight distinct, currently available technologies that such countries could employ:

> Many countries, such as North Korea, Iran and Iraq probably would rely initially on readily available technology—including separating RVs [re-entry vehicles], spin-stabilized RVs, RV reorientation, radar absorbing material, booster fragmentation, low-power jammers, chaff, and simple (balloon) decoys—to develop penetration aids and countermeasures.

Moreover, foreign espionage and other collection efforts are likely to increase, says the National Intelligence Estimate. This would increase the likelihood that adversary nations could use such critical information to improve their ability to overcome U.S. defenses.

These "readily available technologies" could present severe problems for any missile interceptor. Again, these are not new technologies. An analysis prepared by the Office of Technology Assessment in 1988 confirmed that:

- There are plausible decoy designs that would be very difficult to counter merely with passive infrared sensors in conjunction with radar.
- It appears possible that chaff, if properly deployed with decoys, could be used to deny RV detection and more easily, deny RF [radio frequency] discrimination to the radar elements of a defense.
- Whereas chaff would deny information to radar, aerosols would mask RVs and decoys from infrared sensors.

In a review of sensor systems under consideration in 1987, including the ground-launched Probe system and the satellite-based Space Surveillance and Tracking System (the predecessor of the Space-Based Infrared System now planned), the Defense Science Board also noted: "Serious questions remain unanswered about the ability of the passive IR [infra-red] sensors on Probe and SSTS to carry out discrimination against anything but the most primitive decoys and debris. In addition, the presence of cooled RVs would greatly reduce the range of proposed sensors." These serious questions remain today.

## RESOURCES

Perhaps the most extensive work on countermeasures now available to the general public is the study by the Union of Concerned Scientists and the Massachusetts Institute of Technology Security Studies Program, "Countermeasures: A Technical Evaluation of the Operational Effectiveness of the Planned US National Missile Defense System." For access, see Resources in Chapter Four.

# Appendix Two

# Waste, Fraud, and Abuse

National policy forbids classification of material because of "waste, fraud, and abuse." Chapters One and Five note two examples of such abuse that have adversely affected the national policy and foreign relations of the United States. One is the misrepresentation, by Lawrence Livermore National Laboratory, of the nuclear bomb–driven X-ray laser program that was responsible for the genesis of "Star Wars" in the 1980s. The second is the current National Missile Defense program. This appendix examines each example in more detail.

## THE X-RAY LASER

In an op-ed piece in the *New York Times*, Edward Teller claimed responsibility for having introduced President Ronald Reagan to a strategic defense program based on the X-ray laser. Others believe that this was a false trail laid down by Reagan's aides, and, in particular, by Robert McFarlane, who thought that if the Strategic Defense Initiative could be used as a bargaining chip with the Soviet Union, it would be the "greatest sting operation in history."

The following facts are known: The X-ray laser was prominent in the seven-volume October 1983 report by the Defensive Technologies Study Team, headed by James C. Fletcher, former head of the National Aeronautics and Space Administration. This report, commonly referred to as the Fletcher Report, was produced in response to "National Security Study Directive 6–83," a presidential directive dated April 18, 1983. The optimism expressed in the Executive Summary of the Fletcher report regarding the future of a system based on the X-ray laser bears little relation to the contents of the seven volumes; in particular, the countermeasures volume was devastating.

By 1985, Roy Woodruff, who had been Livermore's associate director for defense programs, was fully aware that the measurements of X-ray laser brightness and claims for effectiveness were seriously flawed.[1] Woodruff attempted to get the director of Livermore Laboratory, Roger Batzel, to curb the Washington lobbying of Edward Teller and his protégé, Lowell Wood. In an October 19, 1985, memo, Woodruff wrote that policy makers of the administration had been given information that had not been reviewed by him, and that was "potentially misleading." In particular, he warned, misleading information had been given to the highest levels of the government, including the president's science advisor; the director of central intelligence; the national security advisor; Ambassador Paul Nitze, the president's advisor on arms control; and the president himself. Woodruff wrote, "I have been faced with a dilemma. Do I remain relatively silent and allow Lowell [Wood] to continue to potentially mislead the highest levels of leadership in the country? That would certainly be the easy course of action as you have made it clear on numerous occasions that you[r] preference is for me to do nothing."

An example of what Woodruff was talking about was included in a letter from Edward Teller to Ambassador Paul Nitze, dated December 28, 1984. In it Teller states:

> [A] single x-ray laser module the size of an executive desk which applied this technology could potentially shoot down the entire Soviet land-based missile force, if it were to be launched into the module's field-of-view. . . . It might be possible to generate as many as 100,000 independently aimable beams from a single x-ray laser module.

In an earlier December 22, 1983, letter to George Keyworth, then science advisor to the president, Teller stated that the X-ray laser was "now entering the engineering phase," and that a supplemental appropriation of $100 million in 1985 was needed. He finally got the money when he claimed, in a September 6, 1985, meeting in the Pentagon called by General Abrahamson, who headed the "Star Wars" program, that "President Reagan told me I could have it."

It is worth quoting Congressman George E. Brown on Teller's claim that the X-ray laser was entering the engineering phase in 1983. Congressman Brown said, when commenting on a 1988 General Accounting Office report on the "Accuracy of Statements Concerning DOE's X-Ray Laser Research Program": "To the weapons community, saying that something is ready to enter engineering means that essentially all of the scientific questions had been solved. Dr. Teller made this statement more than five years ago, yet Excalibur is nowhere near the engineering phase even today."

On November 3, 1987, W. Lowell Morgan, who had been a physicist in R-Program (the X-ray laser project at Livermore Laboratory) during its first four years, and a project leader for atomic modeling of nuclear driven X-ray lasers during his last two years in the program, wrote a letter to Congressman Brown explaining why he quit the program. There were two reasons:

> The first is that I felt that the program was going nowhere; the experiments were very difficult yielding minuscule returns of poor quality data (by conventional standards in physical science) for a tremendous investment of effort and, in my opinion, an obscene investment of money. The second reason is that I felt that the interpretation and presentation of the few scientific results that we had was fraudulent. I might note that R-Program is the laughing stock of the technical staff at the Laboratory—I am certainly not alone in my technical assessment of the program.

Despite these and other misrepresentations, there was no "moment of truth" for "Star Wars," although the nature of the program gradually changed.

## NATIONAL MISSILE DEFENSE

MIT's Dr. Theodore A. Postol's allegation that there were similar misrepresentations of the technology upon which National Missile Defense depends is contained in letters written to President Clinton and to White House Chief of Staff John Podesta.[2] Following these letters, President Clinton decided to delay a decision on the deployment of National Missile Defense based on his application of a set of criteria, including the technical capacity of the system.

Comments quoted in the June 9, 2000, issue of the *New York Times* by Michael W. Munn, a retired Lockheed scientist and a pioneer in anti-missile defense, should set the stage for the reading of letters: "The only way to make it work is to dumb it down. There's no other way to do it. Discrimination has always been the No. 1 problem, and it will always remain that way." He added that manipulation of anti-ballistic missile flight tests was nothing new: "It's always been a wicked game."

### LETTER FROM DR. THEODORE A. POSTOL, PROFESSOR OF SCIENCE, TECHNOLOGY AND NATIONAL SECURITY POLICY, MIT, TO PRESIDENT WILLIAM JEFFERSON CLINTON, JULY 6, 2000

"Dear President Clinton:

I am writing to alert you to a severe information gap among your top advisers that urgently requires closing before your upcoming decision on whether to begin deployment of a National Missile Defense (NMD). The White House staff, the National Security Council, and the Pentagon leadership are failing to provide accurate technical information on NMD, and I urge you to form an independent commission of specialized scientists who are technically literate in this field to provide the critical factual input this decision requires. You should be aware of a series of bald misstatements of verifiable scientific fact about missile defense technology in general, and the current National Missile Defense in particular, issued by your top advisers, including Secretary of Defense Cohen, the Undersecretary of Defense for Policy, Mr. Slocombe, the Undersecretary for Acquisition, Dr. Gansler, and the Head of the Ballistic Missile Defense Organization, Lieutenant General Kadish. A review of these statements collectively and individually leads to several unfortunate but inescapable conclusions:

1. That your senior staff is not in a position to provide you with sound technical advice on a matter vital to the security of the United States.

2. That senior Defense Department officials have been prone to repeated and egregious misstatements of scientific facts about missile defense, some of which are summarized below.

3. That their misstatements have had the effect, which I argue was deliberate on the part of some Pentagon officials, of misleading and suppressing vitally important informed debate on NMD deployment, including consistent error on the side of claiming the NMD system has the ability to discriminate between warheads and decoys, when in fact it does not, and a consistent pattern of spurious objections to alternatives such as boost-phase defenses.

The scientific community and other observers in the US and abroad increasingly feel the integrity and credibility of the deployment decision process has been endangered by this situation. It can be rescued by taking the following steps:

1. Convening a panel of qualified scientific advisors who are truly qualified to assess the scientific and technical merits of NMD and alternative proposals objectively. These advisors should be selected

for their professional accomplishments, independence from the Pentagon and interested parties in the defense industry, and freedom from political considerations, which now threatens to overwhelm substantive debate on NMD deployment.

2. Authorize an investigation of multiple acts of scientific fraud in the National Missile Defense program detailed and documented in a letter I submitted to the White House Chief of Staff, John Podesta, 11 May 2000, and delay deciding on any NMD deployment until after the charges have been investigated and adjudicated with due diligence. The acts of fraud in question have a direct bearing on NMD deployment because they were aimed at concealing serious performance shortfalls in a National Missile Defense System, which is supposed to defend American citizens from nuclear attack.

My May 11 letter to the White House put forth evidence of scientific fraud in the National Missile Defense Program that was subsequently picked up by the *New York Times*. The *Times* reported on 18 May that Lt. Col. Richard Lehner, spokesman for the Ballistic Missile Defense Organization (BMDO), stated that a "detailed written response" to the information and analysis in my letter was being prepared for the White House and for me.

But two months and much national media coverage later, no such response has been forthcoming, and neither the White House staff, the National Security Council, nor the Pentagon has yet to take any visible steps to investigate this matter or to rebut the charges in any way other than rhetorically. Instead the Administration has announced it will take a decision on initial NMD deployment in the next few weeks, without substantively responding to these charges. Even the rhetorical indirect response has been faulty; in recent weeks members of the Pentagon leadership have made numerous technologically illiterate and highly misleading statements about the National Missile Defense program.

The question of the competence of high-level Pentagon officials in the sensitive field of missile defense is of even greater concern to me than the question of dampening important public debate. Their numerous misstatements bespeak basic ignorance of well-known technical facts of direct relevance to the performance of missile defense systems and your deployment decision.

For example, during a June 20 press conference, called in part to deflect criticisms raised in my letter to the White House of May 11, Dr. Jacques Gansler, Undersecretary for Acquisition, Technology & Logistics, who during the press conference claimed forty years of experience in missile defense, made the stunning claim that the National Missile Defense X-band radar was capable of measuring the mass of objects in the near vacuum of space. But even very light objects will behave essentially like heavy ones when observed at high-altitudes in the near vacuum of space. Since one of the critical flaws in the NMD system is the difficulty of operating at such high altitudes, Dr. Gansler's comments seem more than just a random gap in knowledge; it goes to the heart of the matter, namely, pretending the system has the capability to distinguish between warheads and decoys in space, when in fact, as I have stated to the media and documented for the White House, it does not.

During the same conference, Lieutenant General Ronald Kadish, the Director of the Ballistic Missile Defense Organization, was also present and also made a series of assertions that displayed ignorance of basic technical knowledge central to an informed evaluation of NMD. He asserted, for example, that a large 2.2-meter diameter balloon used in the IFT-5 National Missile Defense test was "representative" of the expected decoy threat. It is known that such a balloon would be much brighter than the mock warhead that is being used in the IFT-5 experiment, and could be distinguished from the warhead, provided the kill vehicle has been pre-programmed to home on the dimmest point of light that it sees. But this orchestrated laboratory scenario is hardly "representative" of field conditions, and does not in any way demonstrate usable discrimination capability. To assert otherwise shows fatal ignorance of the fundamental technical problems involved in discriminating among objects in space.

Even in an unrealistic scenario in which an adversary used only 2.2 meter diameter balloons, missile defense could still be defeated easily, simply by deploying multiple balloons while putting a warhead inside one of them. General Kadish's assumption that an enemy would be so incompetent as to fail to realize this even though it had already demonstrated the ability to build ICBMs and light-compact nuclear warheads is a dangerous one to let stand, and still more dangerous to Americans if such thinking forms part of the input into your NMD deployment decision.

Dr. Gansler also postulated that an enemy would be so technically incompetent as to attempt to mislead an NMD kill vehicle with decoys which would "make things . . . look alike in all . . . characteristics," whereas it is clear an adversary could confuse the NMD system by simply making all deployed objects look different to it. This is easily done with large balloons of different size, coating, and temperature, concealing warheads in some balloons and while leaving others empty. Again, the misstatement goes to the heart of the technological deficiency of NMD, its failure to discriminate.

Dr. Gansler has stated his belief that improvements in "software" will somehow make it possible to solve such discrimination problems in the future. But the simple truth, which any competent engineer or scientist understands, is "garbage in, garbage out." No information can be extracted where there is none. If there is no reliable information in the signals created by warheads and decoys tumbling in space, if they have been disguised so as to emit signals that belie their physical characteristics, sophisticated software to interpret those signals will make no difference whatsoever.

Dr. Gansler and General Kadish have also made contradictory and/or misleading statements about alternatives to NMD that the Pentagon under their leadership declined to even consider until public pressure forced them to acknowledge these options, such as boost-phase defenses. For example, they asserted that US intelligence might not be capable of providing information to a land-based boost-phase missile defense about whether or not an enemy missile is an ICBM carrying a nuclear warhead or a large rocket simply launching a satellite. This contradicts their expressions of high confidence that US intelligence will be able to furnish detailed information on whether decoys are being carried by an enemy ICBM, what kind of decoys they are, and how the signals from these decoys will be distinct from those of enemy warheads.

Again, I must point out the consistent pattern wherein each of these misstatements tends in the same overall direction—falsely asserting NMD's ability to discriminate, while steering debate away from a favorable assessment of alternatives such as boost-phase defenses. These misstatements by the two Pentagon officials with the most direct responsibility for assessing NMD technology may help explain related misstatements of fact about NMD technology by higher officials who depend on them for their information, including the Pentagon's Undersecretary of Defense for Policy, Walter Slocombe, and Secretary of Defense Cohen.

The *New York Times* reported June 14 that Secretary Cohen "asserted that it would be hard to develop . . . interceptor[s] that could distinguish between a missile's flame and the missile itself." This contradicts the Department of Defense's own technical simulations of missile hard-body and exhaust-plume signals. In fact, Department of Defense analyses show that by choosing sensors that operate at wavelengths in the Medium Wave Infrared (MWIR), it is relatively straightforward for modern staring sensors to observe both the plume and hard-body of an ICBM in powered flight.

Mr. Slocombe, has stated his belief that North Korea, a country with a Gross Domestic Product roughly equal to that of Paraguay, can build an ICBM in five years, even though it would require a vast industrial base, cadres of scientists and technicians, and the design and implementation of major new rocket motor and airframe subsystems relative to those used in its current short-range/small-payload ballistic missiles. He further asserts that the US, which has had the technology to build huge, fast, and high-acceleration rockets for nearly forty years, cannot build such rockets in a similar time-frame.

These are just a few examples of many fatally misinformed claims which indicate your senior staff is not fielding sufficient technical expertise for an informed deployment decision, and to underscore the need for you to bring in an independent team of scientists to provide you with sound technical advice on a decision so critical to our national security. I don't ask you to take my own word for it but urge you to form a truly independent team of specialized scientists who can cut through the political haze obscuring the NMD debate with scientific facts.

The *New York Times* reported July 5 on growing skepticism and division within the State Department, the Pentagon and inside the CIA on forthcoming intelligence assessments of the missile threat from abroad. At a time when informed dissent on NMD is rising against the danger of a misinformed deployment decision, it is becoming plausible to greater numbers of observers that a discernible pattern in these public misstatements by your senior advisers may also constitute misinformation. It is critical to the integrity of the deployment decision process that even the appearance of misinformation or suppression of public debate be convincingly redressed before the deployment decision goes forward.

By the same token, the credibility of the process cannot survive even the appearance of the White House and Pentagon staff countenancing evidence of major fraud in the National Missile Defense Program, and I urge you to investigate charges of rigged NMD testing detailed in previous correspondence without delay.

Of the three prior letters I wrote to the White House about fraud and mismanagement in the National Missile Defense Program, and about government misuse of the classification system, all have gone unanswered.

The first of these letters was sent on May 11 and provided detailed information and documentation indicating scientific fraud in the National Missile Defense Program. The second, dated 19 May, informed the White House that my letter of May 11 had been classified SECRET by the Pentagon, indicating that the Pentagon either mistakenly declassified documents used by me in my letter to the White House, or as I believe more likely, improperly tried to use the classification system to suppress allegations of waste, fraud, and abuse. There is as yet no indication that this matter is being seriously investigated to determine which is the case. The third letter sent June 26 describes mishandling of classified materials by government officials. Three agents of the Defense Security Service came unannounced to my office at MIT to present me with a classified letter which—in direct violation of standard security procedures—was transported unwrapped and presented to me in a public place. I refused to read it under these circumstances, which could plausibly be construed as an attempt to silence my criticism with intimidation and/or entrapment. I believe these occurrences represent an effort within the Pentagon, apparently with the knowledge and approval of the Assistant Secretary of Defense for C3I [Command, Control, Communications, and Intelligence], Mr. Arthur Money, to dampen any further discussion of the technical merits and demerits of NMD, and to avoid rebuttal of the accusations of scientific fraud in the NMD tests.

There is as yet no indication from the White House that any of these matters is being seriously investigated. If the Administration failed to address these serious, highly publicized, evidence of waste, fraud, abuse and bureaucratic misconduct before it makes its deployment decision, the White House would in effect be encouraging a cynical belief that such practices are countenanced in the Executive Branch.

Here for your convenience is a brief summary of key facts and analysis laid out in the previous letters:

- Top management of the Ballistic Missile Defense Organization sponsored a study that was misrepresented as independent and used to halt an investigation of fraud in the National Missile Defense Program. The Department of Defense Inspector General used this study as an excuse to derail an investigation that had already uncovered substantial evidence of scientific fraud.

- The study continues to be misrepresented by the Ballistic Missile Defense Organization as independent, when in fact it was performed by contractors who worked for, and were paid and supervised by top level BMDO management. This arrangement cannot be considered an independent study and the White House and the Department of Defense Inspector General must not countenance its characterization as such.

- The contractors who claimed to have performed the "independent" analysis of the experimental results [of] the IFT-1A flight test removed and concealed data from that test that did not support their stated conclusion about the Kill Vehicle's ability to discriminate between decoys and warheads.

  The willful concealment of experimental data that does not support the conclusions of a scientific study based on experiment meets the legal definition of fraud.

- The contractors also selectively altered analysis parameters in the remaining unconcealed data to create the false impression that the combination of measured data and theory together supported their conclusions.

  The altered analysis parameters were the expected infrared signal intensities from objects observed in the earth exo-atmosphere during the IFT-1A experiment.

  These parameters were supposed to be derived from basic physical principles and scientific analysis, and were supposed to demonstrate the scientific capacity to predict how objects in space will look to Kill Vehicle sensors.

Concealing the alteration of these parameters is fraudulent, as it conceals the fact that the theory and experimental data were incompatible and could not be used to accurately predict what the Kill Vehicle would see in combat.

- Following the revelations that almost all of the decoys flown in the the IFT-1A experiment could deceive the Kill Vehicle, the BMDO altered the entire flight test program from IFT-3 to 18 to conceal the fact that the Kill Vehicle could not deal with simple decoys.

  This was done by removing all the decoys that created discrimination problems in the IFT-1A experiment, just as data that did not support the findings of the fraudulent BMDO "independent" study was removed.

It is clear that each of the actions described above could not have been taken without knowledge, careful deliberation, and forethought. It is equally clear that these actions were designed to conceal serious technical problems in the program, and that the BMDO top management was the primary coordinator of these actions, including the actions of contractors who were under BMDO management.

One does not need to be trained as a lawyer to see that elements of fraud [are] present in the actions listed above, although lawyers tell me more specifically they may be covered under the broadly worded statute on fraud and false statements, USCA Section 1001. Credible evidence of coordinated actions by BMDO top-level management to conceal information that did not support their claims, knowledge of the concealment of this information by the top levels of BMDO management, and claims made that would not otherwise be supported by the facts may well constitute actionable evidence of fraud, and they warrant action before the deployment decision.

This evidence does not point merely to honest differences of opinion among scientists and engineers, nor does it constitute a mere political flap to be tamped down with "spin control." To tacitly allow it to pass as such would not only promote an environment where both bad government and irresponsible executive management can flourish, but it also directly threatens our national security as you approach your deployment decision.

The tight schedule the White House has chosen for a decision on NMD deployment is all the more reason to investigate these charges immediately. Had the White House acted two months ago to form a team of independent scientists to examine the questions raised here, I believe the matter could have been resolved by now. Instead, lack of competent and politicized scientific advice has blocked substantive progress toward an informed decision. I know for a fact that one of the country's most distinguished scientists who heads an important advisory group to the Administration has told Leon Fuerth, the Vice President's National Security Advisor, that he agrees with the concerns presented in my letter of 11 May, and still no visible action was taken.

I stand ready to serve the Administration in any way I can to help investigate and resolve these matters responsibly. Once again I urge in the strongest terms the immediate formation of an independent advisory commission of accomplished scientists who are independent of the Pentagon, and prompt investigation of the allegations of fraud and misconduct detailed above, before any initial deployment decision is made.

### LETTER FROM MR. JOHN PODESTA, WHITE HOUSE CHIEF OF STAFF, TO DR. THEODORE A. POSTOL, JULY 14, 2000

Dear Dr. Postol:

Thank you for your letters on national missile defense. The Department of Defense will be responding to you separately.

I want to assure you that the President will take into account all available information before making a decision on NMD deployment based on the four criteria he has set forth: threat, cost, technical feasibility, and national security, including arms control. The concerns you have raised regarding the ability of our proposed NMD system to engage effectively ballistic missiles with countermeasures is and will be an important issue in our review of the technical feasibility of our NMD.

Finally, regarding the visit of representatives of the Defense Security Service, let me assure you that you are not under investigation, as the Department of Defense has already explained to you.

### LETTER FROM DR. THEODORE A. POSTOL TO MR. JOHN PODESTA, JULY 21, 2000

Dear Mr. Podesta:

I am writing you in response to what is close to a form letter from you dated 14 July 2000. This letter appears to be your response to information you have been sent indicating both government fraud and misconduct in relation to the National Missile Defense Program and attempts of government officials to improperly use the security and classification system to suppress public discussion on this matter.

With regard to your comments on the improper conduct of agents of the Defense Security Service, please rest assured that my letters to you on that matter were not motivated by any concerns I had, or have, about my being investigated. Instead they were motivated by my concern that you and other staff at the White House could properly be held accountable for not dealing with such matters of fraud and misconduct.

The almost comically unresponsive letter you sent to me more than two months after being informed about these serious matters adds to my concern that you and others on the White House staff have not taken your responsibilities seriously—and of much greater importance—have not taken responsible action to deal with the very serious issues raised in the letters sent to you.

I sincerely hope that this is only a wrong impression created by a badly drafted and inadvertently unresponsive letter, rather than a true indication of the actual flaws of how you and the White House staff are dealing with such serious matters related to our national security and attempts to tamper with the democratic process.

Those interested in the scientific issues involved in Dr. Postol's charges will want to read the following earlier letter to Mr. John Podesta. The letter describes the attachments that contain the detailed technical arguments. Only excerpts from Attachment A are included, the others being too voluminous and technical to allow inclusion here.

### LETTER FROM DR. THEODORE POSTOL TO MR. JOHN PODESTA, MAY 11, 2000

I am writing to alert you to information that is of profound importance to President Clinton's impending decision on whether to deploy the currently under development National Missile Defense system. I have obtained and analyzed the Ballistic Missile Defense Organization's (BMDO's) own published data from the Integrated Flight Test-1A (IFT-1A) and have discovered that the BMDO's own data shows that the Exoatmospheric Kill Vehicle (EKV) will be defeated by the simplest of balloon decoys. I also have documentation that shows that the BMDO in coordination with its contractors attempted to hide this fact by tampering with both the data and analysis from the IFT-1A experiment. In addition, it appears that the BMDO modified the configuration of the IFT-2, 3, and 4 follow-on flight tests to hide the program-stopping facts revealed in the IFT-1A. The documentation and analysis that supports my claims are attached to this letter as Attachments A through D.

In the remainder of this letter I will briefly summarize the findings documented in the four attachments.

Attachments A and B explain how the BMDO's own data from the IFT-1A test shows that the BMDO falsely represented the results of the IFT-1A test as showing that an Exoatmospheric Kill Vehicle (EKV) can tell warheads from simple balloon decoys. It is easy to understand this result from a simple explanation of how the EKV works (see Attachments A and B for further details).

The EKV sees both decoys and warheads as unresolved points of light, and it attempts to find warheads by examining how each point of light fluctuates in time. The intensity of the signal from each potentially lethal object depends on its size, temperature, surface materials and spatial orientation, and the fluctuation in the signal from each object depends on how its orientation changes in time. The data from the IFT-1A experiment showed that the changing spatial orientation of the decoys and warheads as they fell through the near vacuum of space was nearly the same, each resulting in a signal that fluctuated in a varied and totally unpredictable way. Consequently, the IFT-1A data showed that there was no fluctuating feature in the signals from decoys and warheads that could be used to distinguish one object from the other.

One of the early post-flight manifestations of this fact was immediately evident when the BMDO review of the telemetry data from the IFT-1A flight test resulted in the defense system always wrongly identifying a partially inflated balloon as the mock warhead. The team performing the post-flight analysis dealt with this failure by simply removing the balloon from the data, as if it was never there.

Even after removing the balloon, the post-flight experimental data still showed that two other benign objects were *brighter* than the warhead and therefore were judged more likely to be the mock warhead. The team performing the post-flight experiment analysis dealt with this outcome by arbitrarily rejecting the data from the time interval where the two other objects were brighter, and instead chose without technical reason a second time period where the warhead was brighter due to the accident of its spatial orientation. This elaborate hoax was then screened by describing this tampering with the data and analysis in terms of misleading, confusing, and self contradictory language—to create the false impression that the results were supported by well established scientific methods.

In truth, the procedures followed by the BMDO were like rolling a pair of dice and throwing away all outcomes that did not give snake eyes, and then fraudulently making a claim that they have scientific evidence to show that they could reliably predict when a roll of the dice will be a snake eyes.

These meretricious procedures used by the analysis team were applied because the IFT-1A data revealed that the signals from some of the decoys in the experiment were essentially indistinguishable from that of the mock warhead. Stated differently, the signals from both the warhead and balloons had no features that could be exploited to tell one from the other using credible scientific methods—so the team invented a set of fraudulent methods to get the desired result.

In view of the results of the IFT-1A experiment, it is now clear why the

IFT-2, 3, and 4 experiments were re-configured following the analysis of IFT-1A.

After the IFT-1A experiment, the BMDO changed the number of objects it planned to fly in follow-on experiments from ten to four. The four objects were to be a medium reentry vehicle (MRV), a 2.2 meter diameter balloon, and two balloons of diameter 0.6 meters.

Some time after this reduction in the number of objects to be flown in IFT-2, 3, and 4 experiments, the number of objects was again changed. This time the two 0.6 meter balloons were removed, because of the high probability that the seeker would mistake one of them for the mock warhead. This action further reduced the number of objects for the IFT-2, 3, and 4 follow-on experiments from four to two, leaving only a single large balloon and a medium warhead.

The fidelity of the IFT-2, 3, and 4 experiments was further undermined by the BMDO through the careful choice of a time of day for the intercept attempt, which placed the sun behind the EKV illuminating the balloon and warhead from the front. In this experimental geometry, the willful insertion of the 2.2 meter diameter balloon converted it from what otherwise might have been a credible decoy to an object that was unambiguously a beacon. In addition, the very large differences in the intensity between the balloon and warhead made it easy to distinguish between the two targets—while at the same time making it easier for the EKV to home on the dimmer but still very bright warhead near the balloon.

The results of the IFT-1A experiment, and the way it was allowed to influence the modifications to the IFT-2, 3, and 4 experiments, is of profound significance for the President's decision on whether or not to move forward with the current National Missile Defense concept, as it is now clear that the entire concept relies on a flawed analysis of the most basic and critical flight test data. When the data from these experiments are properly analyzed and interpreted, they indicate that the current NMD system will not be able to reliably deal with even the most simple first generation countermeasures. Such trivially simple countermeasures could include the use of tumbling warheads, partially inflated balloon decoys, and decoys and warheads constructed with tethered objects and "rabbit-ear" type appendages.

The points made herein can be readily verified by a careful review of the study *"Independent Review of TRW Discrimination Techniques Final Report (POET Study 1998–5)."* This document (included here as Attachment D) contains a mix of irrelevant and profound findings about the post-flight analysis of the telemetry data, creating a superficial but false impression of a sound scientific analysis. A careful reading of this report and the related documents included in the attachments instead reveals the following:

*Data that demonstrated that the EKV would always mistake a partially inflated balloon for the mock lethal object was inexplicably removed from the post-flight analysis of the EKV's performance.

*After this data was removed, the data from the eight other remaining benign objects and the lethal mock warhead showed that the system would still mistakenly choose two of the benign objects instead of the lethal object.

*In order to alter this unfavorable outcome, the team tampered with both the data and the analysis of the data to artificially create a false outcome where the system would choose the mock warhead.

This highly organized and systematic pattern of actions has the appearance of an elaborate scientific and technical blunder, which urgently needs to be investigated by a team of scientists who are recognized for their scientific accomplishments and independence from the Pentagon. Fortunately, the physical phenomena and analysis techniques at issue here are well known to many highly skilled independent scientists who work on problems in basic physics, computer science, and in the analysis of statistical data, so assembling a team of top-notch independent scientists who can evaluate the BMDO's analytical claims should be no problem.

I urge the White House to put together such a team of scientists who can independently evaluate the procedures used to reach these erroneous conclusions about the content of the telemetry data from the IFT-1A flight test and the subsequent modifications of the IFT-2, 3, and 4 flight tests.

Attachments A, B, C, and D contain detailed explanations of the findings provided in this letter along with the documentation from which they are derived.

### Excerpts from Attachment A: Explanation of Why the Sensor in the Atmospheric Kill Vehicle (EKV) Cannot Reliably Discriminate Decoys from Warheads

The Integrated Flight Test 1A (IFT-1A) was a very critical test of the sensor technology that is to be used in the Exoatmospheric Kill Vehicle (EKV). Its purpose was to flyby a complex of ten targets to gather "signature" information on objects that were deployed in space, and to use this signature information to determine how effective the kill vehicle sensor will be in identifying warheads that are mixed in with light decoys. Ten targets were used in the IFT-1A experiment—one mock warhead, and nine balloons of various size, shape, and surface coatings.

Each of the targets contained instruments that measured and reported their location in space. In addition, as the kill vehicle sensor platform coasted towards the complex of targets, data on all objects in the sensor's field of view was transmitted to the ground for post-flight analysis.

Thus, the IFT-1A experiment was a highly controlled and instrumented

experiment designed to collect sensor data on objects that were fully characterized and traveling through space. The subsequent analysis of the IFT-
1A data was then supposed to be used to evaluate how effective the EKV
sensor would be against objects where their detailed characteristics are un-
known.

For reasons that will be described in *Attachment B*, subsequent analysis of
*the sensor data from the IFT-1A experiment reveals that the sensor data contains
essentially no information that uniquely identifies the warhead.* As a result, the
EKV has a very low probability of selecting warheads among decoys.

The IFT-1A experiment simply showed that the physical motions of light
and heavy objects in the near vacuum of space are sufficiently similar that
objects cannot be selected by simply measuring the fluctuations in their
brightness as they tumble, spin, and/or precess. Stated differently, light and
heavy objects will tumble, spin, and/or precess in the same way as long as
they have the same distribution of mass (more accurately, as long as the light
and heavy objects have the same ratios of moments of inertia, they will have
the same physical dynamics in space).

Thus very simple decoys will predictably have the effect of drastically
reducing the probability of intercept of the current National Missile Defense, resulting in a defense that could readily be defeated by the most technologically primitive of adversaries.

### How the Exoatmospheric Kill Vehicle (EKV) Picks Its Target

The Exoatmospheric Kill Vehicle contains a telescope that can observe
targets in the visible and at least two infrared wavelengths. The exact resolution of the telescope is classified, but it is easy to show that it should have
an angular resolution of roughly 150 to 300 microradians. This means that
the resolution of the EKV against objects at 1000 kilometers range is between 150 and 300 meters, and even at 10 kilometers range, the resolution
will be roughly 1.5 to 3 meters.

When the EKV is 3 to 6 kilometers from a target, it has less than half a
second to maneuver before impact with the target. At this point in the homing process, the EKV has either picked the right target or it has failed.

Since the EKV must pick the target it is to home against many tens of
seconds prior to impact, it must be able to identify both warheads and decoys
at ranges of many hundreds of kilometers. As a result, all objects simply
appear like points of light to the EKV during the time it must determine
which objects are warheads and which are decoys.

\* \* \*

In summary, the EKV sees targets as only fluctuating points of light. The
fluctuations in the signal from targets are due to changes in their orienta-

Large Balloon
With Reflecting Coating

2.2 Meter Diameter Balloon
With Black Coating

Balloon With White Coating

Light Rigid Replica Decoy

Minuteman Inflatable Decoy

Minuteman Warhead

The IEO, an inflatable erectable decoy for Minuteman
(L'Garde, Inc. Photo)

Mk 12A Minuteman III Reentry Vehicle

Figure 2. Examples of objects that could appear to be warheads to the Exoatmospheric Kill Vehicle's sensors.
(Dr. Theodore A. Postol)

tion as they precess, rotate, and/or tumble in space. The absolute magnitude of infrared signals from objects will depend on their temperature, surface coatings, geometry, and size. All of these characteristics can be controlled and altered by an adversary. Thus, the only hope the EKV has to discriminate light decoys from heavy warheads is if the motions of the heavy warheads are different in an identifiable way from the motions of decoys. This will not be the case if the decoys are designed so that the ratio of their moments of inertia are the same. It is also possible to package the warhead in a balloon, so the infrared signal from it cannot be observed, or the infrared signal from the warhead can be modified by tethering objects to the warhead that cannot be resolved by the EKV, but lead to fluctuations in the signal that have nothing to do with the physical characteristics of the warhead. Thus, it is no surprise that even under the highly orchestrated conditions of the IFT-1A experiment, the sensor flyby data showed that for at least some of the objects, there were no features in the data to indicate that they were not the warhead.

### NOTES

1. Problems with the laser brightness measurements were first raised by George Maenchen in an internal Livermore memo, dated April 6, 1984 (COPD 84–92), where he noted that "It may, however, be difficult to correct the rosy impression left by the earlier, exuberant claims." The analysis was contained in another memo, dated April 14, 1984, and titled "ROMANO Power Measurements." ROMANO was a test of the nuclear-pumped X-ray laser that presumably provided the first good evidence of its lasing; the test took place on December 16, 1983. Teller could not help but have been aware of the problems.

2. While most of the discussion in the letters reprinted here concerns the TRW exoatmospheric kill vehicle, the reader should keep in mind that, although the Raytheon design used since 1998 employs different wavelength bands, including the visible, this does not alter the inability of the kill vehicle to discriminate warheads from decoys. As a result, the discussion contained in the excerpts of Attachment A to the second letter, explaining why the exoatmospheric kill vehicle's sensors cannot discriminate decoys from warheads, remains relevant. The other attachments to this letter are omitted here because of their length and highly technical nature.

# Appendix Three

# The Center for International Policy

The Center for International Policy, a Washington, D.C., foreign policy association, believes that military and intelligence programs must be subject to far greater scrutiny to make them more accountable to the American people. Its sponsorship of *The Phantom Defense: America's Pursuit of the Star Wars Illusion* reflects that belief, and is part of its program, lasting nearly three decades, to promote a foreign policy based on democracy, social justice, and human rights.

In the late 1970s, the center led a campaign to set human-rights standards for the distribution of U.S. foreign assistance. The co-chairmen of the center's board were Representative Donald Fraser and Representative (now Senator) Tom Harkin, the principal sponsors of landmark legislation that made the promotion of human rights a stated goal of U.S. foreign policy.

In the 1980s, the center's focus shifted to Central America. U.S. policy was fueling civil wars in El Salvador, Guatemala, and Nicaragua, and the center led efforts in the United States to seek a negotiated regional solution. The center's staff organized U.S. support for the Contadora and Arias peace plans, which culminated in an August 1987 agreement written by President Oscar Arias of Costa Rica and signed by all five Central American presidents.

Robert E. White, former U.S. ambassador to El Salvador, who had taken a stand against the death squads and in favor of a negotiated end to that nation's civil war, became the center's president in 1989. When the Haitian military overthrew the democratically elected president of Haiti in 1991, Ambassador White took up the cause of Haiti's exiled democratic leaders. White led five congressional delegations to Haiti and wrote recommendations for the incoming Clinton administration. A center team accompanied President Jean-Bertrand Aristide and other leaders during the critical negotiations that established legal and diplomatic conditions for the restoration of the constitutional order in Haiti. The center has subsequently followed events closely in Haiti, and pointed out recent falsification of election results.

In 1992 the center established a program to forge a more rational U.S. policy toward Cuba, arguing that the U.S. trade embargo is counterproductive and hurts U.S. economic and political interests. The center's Cuba project holds conferences in the United States and Cuba, and facilitates exchanges between Americans and Cubans to broaden the debate.

In 1993 the center and the Costa Rica–based Arias Foundation organized a joint project to encourage the demilitarization of Central America and the Caribbean. The project initiated a grassroots demilitarization campaign that now has chapters in all of the region's countries. The project has published articles and books, and, in 1998, with the Latin American Working Group, co-published a book entitled *Just the Facts*, which documented U.S. security programs in Latin America and the Caribbean.

In 1995 the center began work on a project to reform U.S. intelligence agencies. Over the following two years, the center sponsored six seminars in congressional hearing rooms on intelligence issues, and sponsored the publication of *National Insecurity: U.S. Intelligence After the Cold War*, which was edited by Craig Eisendrath and published by Temple University Press in 2000.

The center is presently engaged in a national-security project that assesses the role of both intelligence and defense in the formulation and execution of U.S. foreign policy. The center believes that misplaced funding priorities have contributed to the militarization of U.S. foreign policy and reduced public accountability.

In 1999, Ambassador White led a congressional delegation to Colombia to meet with top government officials and with the leaders of the main guerrilla group, the FARC. Center staff members are urging U.S. policy makers in the executive and legislative branches to support the Colombian government's efforts to negotiate a settlement with the guerrillas to end the thirty-year-old civil war.

In 2000, the center launched a program for demilitarization and peacekeeping in Africa. The center has also been active in fostering U.S. adherence to the International Land Mine Convention.

# Index

## About the Authors

CRAIG EISENDRATH is Senior Fellow with the Center for International Policy, a foreign policy institute in Washington, D.C., and a former U.S. Foreign Service Officer with expertise in nuclear and outer space issues. His articles and commentary on foreign affairs have appeared recently in the *Bulletin of Atomic Scientists*, *The Philadelphia Inquirer*, *The Baltimore Sun*, and other publications. He is the editor of *National Insecurity: U.S. Intelligence After the Cold War* (2000).

MELVIN A. GOODMAN is Professor of National Security at the National War College and Senior Fellow at the Center for International Policy. He is also an adjunct professor at American University and Johns Hopkins University. He was a senior Soviet analyst at the Central Intelligence Agency and the State Department from 1966 to 1986. He has authored three books on Russian foreign policy and is editor of *Lessons Learned: The Cold War* (2001).

GERALD E. MARSH, a physicist at Argonne National Laboratory, was a consultant to the Office of the Chief of Naval Operations on strategic nuclear policy and technology for many years. He also served with the U.S. START delegation in Geneva and is on the editorial board of the *Bulletin of the Atomic Scientists*. He is a Fellow of the American Physical Society and has published widely in the areas of weapons technology and foreign policy.